The
Forster–Cavafy Letters

The
Forster–Cavafy
Letters

Friends at a
Slight Angle

Edited and Annotated by
Peter Jeffreys

The American University in Cairo Press
Cairo New York

Copyright © 2009 by
The American University in Cairo Press
113 Sharia Kasr el Aini, Cairo, Egypt
420 Fifth Avenue, New York, NY 10018
www.aucpress.com

Introduction, selection, and notes copyright © 2009 by Peter Jeffreys. Foreword copyright © 2009
by Manuel Savidis. E.M. Forster letters copyright © 2009 by the Provost and Scholars of King's
College, Cambridge. C.P. Cavafy Letters copyright © 2009 by the Cavafy Archive/Manuel Savidis.
George Valassopoulo translations and letter copyright © 2009 by Irene Lightbody. Arnold Toynbee
letter copyright © 2009 by Jean Toynbee. William Plomer letter and poem copyright © 2009 by
William Plomer Trust. Leonard Woolf letters copyright © 2009 by the University of Sussex and the
Society of Authors as the literary representative of the estate of Leonard Woolf. Robert Graves letter
copyright © 2009 by A.P. Watt Ltd on behalf of the Trustees of the Robert Graves Copyright Trust.
Bonamy Dobrée letter copyright © 2009 by David Higham Associates on behalf of the Bonamy
Dobrée estate. E.M. Forster's letter to T.S. Eliot (11 March 1924) published by permission of the
Houghton Library, Harvard University (bMS Am 1432 50).

Dar el Kutub No. 16768/08
ISBN 978 977 416 257 2

Dar el Kutub Cataloging-in-Publication Data

Jeffreys, Peter
    The Forster–Cavafy Letters: Friends at a Slight Angle / Edited and annotated by
    Peter Jeffreys.—Cairo: The AmericanUniversity in Cairo Press, 2008
        p.   cm.
        ISBN 977 416 257 9
        1. Letters—collections   2. Forster, Edward Morgan 1879–1970
        3. Cavafy, C.P. 1863–1933 I. Title
        808.86

1 2 3 4 5 6 7 8   14 13 12 11 10 09

Designed by Fatiha Bouzidi
Printed in Egypt

For Michael

Contents

Cavafy Anthology
Translated by George Valassopoulo

Foreword

This volume of correspondence between E.M. Forster and C.P. Cavafy has been some forty-five years in the making. I am not counting time from the initial written exchange between the two men, ninety-two years ago, or the last one, seventy-seven years ago—rather, I am dating the idea of its publication from 1964, when G.P. Savidis presented E.M. Forster with copies of his letters and Cavafy's drafts.

There have been several attempts at editing and publishing these letters in the five intervening decades. All such attempts were aborted for a variety of reasons which need not be elaborated here; this auspicious occasion calls not for an account of repeated failure, but for a celebration of singular success.

The main reason for this success rests with Dr. Peter Jeffreys. He is a true scholar in the traditional sense of the word: a man of considerable insight, willing and able to make the extra effort that will reveal the details that link cause and effect and shed light on the greater scheme of things.

Dr. Jeffreys presents the Forster–Cavafy letters with abundant annotation and in full context, which means including additional letters to and from at least ten different individuals (such as T.S. Eliot and Robert Graves). The Forster–Cavafy story is thus presented as a fascinating and authoritative narrative, with numerous side stories explored or hinted at for anyone interested in further pursuit.

Links, intertextuality, parallel narratives: this is thought to be the exclusive domain of Web expositions. We tend to forget that the best textual expositions, such as this one, are every bit as impressive and all-encompassing—and even more admirable for the fact that they achieve this without the benefit of smoke, mirrors, or hyperlinks.

My impression is that these letters are presented in the best fashion possible, by the best person for the job, at the best time for a sober appreciation of the singular relationship between E.M. Forster and C.P. Cavafy. Good things sometimes do come to those who wait.

Manuel Savidis
The Cavafy Archive, Athens
11 March 2009

Acknowledgments and Archival Sources

This volume of the E.M. Forster–C.P. Cavafy letters owes much to the efforts and assistance of numerous archivists, librarians, scholars, colleagues, and friends, without whom none of the necessary publishing trajectories would have aligned. Initial encouragement and ongoing support for this project was provided by Manuel Savidis, whose family history is uniquely connected to the story of these letters. His unwavering collaborative assistance has allowed me access to indispensable archival materials. I am equally indebted to the archival expertise and philological talents of Katerina Ghika of the Center of Neo-Hellenic Studies (Cavafy Archive, Athens), who has been involved with this project at every turn and has co-edited the accompanying Valassopoulo translations. Patricia McGuire, the archivist of the Modern Archive Centre at King's College, Cambridge, has provided invaluable assistance with the E.M. Forster material. I am grateful to both the Society of Authors as agents for the Provost and Scholars of King's College, and Manuel Savidis, director of the Cavafy Archive, for permission to publish this long-awaited correspondence. The gracious consent of Irene Lightbody, daughter of the late George Valassopoulo, allowed for the unique opportunity to present her father's extant Cavafy translations alongside the letters. I also thank her for providing photographs of her father and her exquisite painting of the Valassopoulo villa. Eric LaPre, my talented research assistant, has done an extraordinary job in assisting me with the demanding tasks of transcribing, proofreading, and copyediting.

The groundwork for organizing this challenging material was laid out decades ago by the late George Savidis, who long wished to see these letters published in full. The scholarly work of P.N. Furbank and Mary Lago on the main corpus of E.M. Forster's letters has served as the foundation on which my editing and annotating are based. Michael Haag kindly shared his vast knowledge of modern Alexandria and singular familiarity with its legendary cosmopolitanism. I am deeply indebted to these fine scholars for effectively preserving, cataloguing, and researching the materials necessary for the full story of these letters to be told.

Ample thanks are owed the editors at the American University in Cairo Press—Neil Hewison, Randi Danforth, Nadia Naqib, and Abdalla Hassan—for bringing this volume to press. For permission to include supporting letters, I am grateful to Duff Hart-Davis (William Plomer Trust), Jean Toynbee, the University of Sussex and the Society of Authors as the Literary Representative of the Estate of Leonard Woolf, the Houghton Library of Harvard University, A.P. Watt Ltd. on behalf of the Trustees of the Robert Graves Copyright Trust, and David Higham Associates on behalf of the Bonamy Dobrée Estate. The inclusion of unpublished Valassopoulo translations and archival photographs was made possible by permission of the Cavafy Archive and the Modern Archive Centre, King's College, Cambridge. Jacqueline Banerjee generously allowed the inclusion of her photograph of Forster's home at Weybridge, and Sophia Bora of the Hellenic Literary and Historical Archive (ELIA) provided vintage photographs of Alexandria.

Additional thanks are due to the librarians Peter Jones and Elizabeth Ennion-Smith (King's College, Cambridge University), Andrew Grey (Durham University), Rhea Karabelas Lesage and Rachel Howarth (Harvard University), and Kathleen Maio (Suffolk University) for their assistance with manuscripts and sources. Travel grants to Athens and

Cambridge were made available through the generous support of Dean Kenneth Greenberg and Tony Merzlak. Artemis Leontis, Hilary Nanda, Voula Shone, and Michael Tandoc have offered important criticism and helpful comments along the way. To my parents Irene and George I am ever grateful for their ongoing financial and moral support. I thank Elizabeth Haylett Clark, Georgia Glover, Lisa Dowdeswell, Emily Kitchin, Chip Rossetti, and Andrew Butler for their assistance with various fine details integral to the completion of this project.

The letters and poems were transcribed from the following archival sources:

Forster's letters to Cavafy: Cavafy Archive F/44–48
Cavafy's drafts of letters to Forster: Cavafy Archive F/44–48
Letters from Arnold Toynbee and William Plomer to Forster: Cavafy Archive   F/44
Letter from Robert Graves to Forster: Cavafy Archive F/44
Typescripts of Cavafy translations by George Valassopoulo: King's College, Cambridge EMF/18/104; Cavafy Archive F/45/48/99/100
Letters exchanged between George Valassopoulo and Forster: King's College, Cambridge EMF/18/562
E.M. Forster Poems: King's College, Cambridge EMF/8/6, EMF/8/19
Letters exchanged between Cavafy and Leonard Woolf: Cavafy Archive F 74, F 75
Letter from Bonamy Dobrée to Cavafy: Cavafy Archive F/72
Letters exchanged between Forster and Alekos Singopoulo: Cavafy Archive, Singopoulo File
Letters from Forster to George Savidis: Cavafy/Savidis Archive
Letter from Forster to T.S. Eliot: Houghton Library (bMSAm 1432 50)

Introduction

The correspondence of E.M. Forster and C.P. Cavafy documents one of the most intriguing and peculiar literary friendships of the twentieth century. Spanning some fifteen years, the letters bear witness to a rather asymmetrical relationship characterized by both intimate warmth and impersonal detachment. Readers of these letters will no doubt find them entertaining and remarkable for a number of reasons. To begin with, the playfully effusive tone that animates Forster's letters stands in marked contrast to the reserve of Cavafy's laconic replies. This imbalance has as much to do with personalities as it does with political and historical circumstances that factored into the relationship and which will be examined in due course. Temperamentally, both Forster and Cavafy had a knack for letter writing. Forster, as P.N. Furbank informs us, was a faithful and indefatigable correspondent (his surviving letters total some fifteen thousand) who wrote "*for* the particular recipient and with that particular relationship in mind."[1] Cavafy, by contrast, used the epistolary medium more pragmatically to express practical matters, as would be expected from an office clerk professionally trained to supervise and edit official correspondence.[2]

Complicating this apparent disparity is a similar divergence in the textual status of the letters. Whereas Forster's original letters were preserved,

Cavafy's letters survive only in the poet's carefully copied drafts[3] which are fraught with excisions and revisions that lend them a peculiar fragmented quality. Indeed, reading through Cavafy's rough drafts creates an experience akin to that described by the speaker in the poem "In the Month of Athyr": "In the damaged part I see the words . . . 'Him . . . Alexandrian' / Then come three lines much mutilated. / But I can read a few words . . . ." In order to recreate this experience for the reader, Cavafy's drafts have been faithfully reproduced with all their revisions so as to preserve more effectively that quintessentially Cavafian quality of meticulously wrought sentiment. As literary documents, these handwritten copies reflect the poet's notorious obsession with excessive revision, a painstaking writing strategy that effectively delayed the publication of a canonical volume of his poems beyond his lifetime.[4] Forster, on the other hand, writes in the present moment with a more spontaneous expression of thought. His letters, by contrast, come across as seemingly more sincere.

Forster's letters to Cavafy were carefully preserved by the poet in their original state, whereas Cavafy's letters to Forster were most likely burned during one of Forster's moves.[5] Fittingly enough, the disparate status of the remaining sets of letters corresponds quite appropriately to the emotional disconnection that in many ways characterizes the Forster–Cavafy relationship. Although seemingly in sympathy with each other, their friendship was somewhat lopsided and increasingly complicated by ideological, political, and artistic differences. For decades critics have felt that Cavafy and Forster held each other in such high regard that they necessarily exerted a degree of mutual influence.[6] To some degree they held common interests, which included an aesthetic appreciation for beautiful men as well as an intense fixation on Greek culture. A closer reading of the letters, however, reveals a different dynamic altogether. When framed within the complex sociopolitical circumstances under which they were composed, these letters shed much light on Forster's and Cavafy's shared sensibilities as well as on their unspoken differences.

Forster was allegedly introduced to Cavafy on 7 March 1916 by P.N. Furness[7] and in a short span of time he established his characteristic intimate tone with the poet. This may be seen in a letter dated 1 July 1917, where Forster touches upon the rather personal topic of "depravity" and whether an artist should be depraved in order to write (see letter 4). The letter sets up a significant point of contrast between Forster's perennial optimism and Cavafy's ironic pessimism. In fact, these two great modernists were less in sympathy with each other's views than they often revealed. Hence a new context for Forster's apt phrase "standing at a slight angle"; to be sure, Forster and Cavafy stood at slight angles to each other both in terms of the ideology of Hellenism which seemingly united them as humanists, as well as the politics of empire that brought them together during the war. While the polite tone that suffuses their correspondence cannot be discounted (it registers the mutual regard and resilient cordiality that endured throughout their seventeen years of friendship), the fact that Cavafy ultimately withheld what Forster so earnestly sought—official authorization to publish an edition of Cavafy's poems in England—speaks volumes about the poet's unexpressed reservations. Thus their friendship was characterized by a frustrating pattern of bestowing and withholding, both of sincere opinions as well as poetic translations.

One aspect of the Forster–Cavafy friendship that strikes the reader of these letters is the relentless push on Forster's part to launch Cavafy's literary career. As he assured Cavafy almost prophetically in a letter dated 23 June 1924, "I am sure that your work will have a European reputation in the end . . ." (see letter 40). With this very end in mind, Forster embarked on a great promotional campaign that did more for Cavafy than the poet could ever have done for Forster in return. Although Forster's efforts to bring out a volume of Cavafy's poetry in England were never realized during the poet's lifetime, the seeds he planted by strategically placing George Valassopoulo's translations in various periodicals would sprout with John Mavrogordato's first English translation, published by the Hogarth Press in 1951. One wonders how Forster might view the present surfeit of Cavafy translations; whether pleased or simply bewildered by this unparalleled translation of a modern Greek poet into English, he would no doubt feel vindicated as having been the first to fully appreciate the appeal of Cavafy's unmistakable voice in translation.[8] This present translation phenomenon, however, would not have surprised Cavafy, who had his eye firmly fixed on the future rather than on the present. The uncanny historic sensibility that enabled Cavafy to scrutinize history in an almost proleptic manner surely led him to intuit that the 1920s and 1930s were inauspicious times for a full volume of his poetry to appear. In hindsight, one can appreciate the prescience of Cavafy's resolve to withhold his poems, a decision that goes some way toward explaining his behavior with Forster. What seems rather incredible though is the risk he took by foregoing such precious publishing opportunities, a refusal that could easily have cost him Forster's friendship.

What did Forster really hope to accomplish through his relentless promotion of Cavafy? On the one hand, the letters reveal the novelist's unmistakable selflessness and uncommon generosity of spirit, the realization of his famous motto to "only connect the passion with the prose," or in this case, the poetry. Yet there is an unmistakable note of aggressiveness that marks Forster's promotional advocacy of Cavafy, one that may be seen as an extension of his more general exploratory and heuristic relationship with Alexandria itself. Certainly Cavafy, enmeshed within the matrix of British imperial authority that relegated post-1882 Egypt to suzerainty status,[9] sensed this passive-aggressive note and in his own way resisted being appropriated. Inscribed within the relationship, then, is an odd imbalance of power: Forster the famous novelist versus Cavafy the obscure poet; Forster the conscientious objector waiting out the war in Alexandria versus Cavafy the petty office bureaucrat working in the Dantean Third Circle of Irrigation. This unacknowledged but unmistakable inequality goes some way toward explaining the slightly awkward and even obsequious formality that comes through in Cavafy's letters to Forster.

A full appreciation of the letters requires that they be read contrapuntally against the textual contents and publication circumstances of Forster's two books on Alexandria: *Alexandria: A History and a Guide* (1922, 1938, 1961) and *Pharos and Pharillon* (1923). To a great extent, these texts reflect Forster's own need to orient himself in a city where he was, at least initially, quite lost. Forster worked his way through Alexandria with a deliberate methodology, seeking not only to find missing soldiers in his official capacity as Red Cross searcher, but also to recover missing pieces of his emotional and literary life. Forster's initial dislike for Alexandria took a decidedly positive turn after he met Cavafy, through whom he found himself seduced by the invisible history of the city. This history Forster would attempt to chronicle in his prose writings and thus master Alexandrian lore—an impulse inspired by Cavafy's impressive command of history. Forster's historicizing project would extend to Cavafy as well, who found himself duly contextualized within the pages of *Pharos and Pharillon*. The presence of Cavafy's poems in these two books contributed greatly to their success, as Forster acknowledged to Cavafy on numerous occasions.

Cavafy would prove to be an important source of artistic rejuvenation for Forster, whose debt to him during this critical period in his life explains the novelist's subsequent loyalty and unflagging dedication to the older poet. As Wilfred Stone notes, Forster's war-time writings "show the novelist reemerging, filling his notebooks and renewing his energies"; and through his encounter with Cavafy, he acquired a "broadmindedness toward the sensuality of the Orient" that propelled him forward.[10] This broadmindedness notwithstanding, Cavafy's decadent celebration of hedonism would remain too excessive for Forster, whose view of "depravity" differed radically from the poet's highly aesthetic celebration of tragic decline and dignified defeat.

Forster initially had trouble adjusting to the "spurious" Levantine East, especially since, to his mind, it compared less favorably to India. In a revealing letter written to Malcolm Dowling on 6 August 1916, Forster confesses his difficulty as a westerner attempting to comprehend Egypt:

I hate the place, or rather its inhabitants. This is interesting, isn't it, because I came inclined to be pleased and quite free from racial prejudices, but in 10 months I've acquired an instinctive dislike to the Arab voice, the Arab figure, the Arab way of looking or walking or pump shitting or eating or laughing or anything—exactly the emotion that I censured in the Anglo-Indian towards the native there. What does this mean? Am I old, or is it the war, or are these people intrinsically worse? Any how I better understand the Anglo-Indian irritation though I'm glad to say I'm as far as ever from respecting it!! It's damnable and disgraceful, and it's in me.[11]

Although this rather disturbing confession confirms Forster's determination to experience the East without colonial prejudice, it also betrays the serious challenges he faced when trying to realize this unbiased ideal. Throughout his career, Forster would continually strive to master what today would be criticized as Orientalist proclivities. His stay in Egypt was marked by this struggle against western attitudes and by other conflicts as well. For the war had induced an uncharacteristic sense of despair in him. With the incompletion of *A Passage to India*, his writing was at a critical standstill, and he had yet to experience a fulfilling sexual relationship. By turning to journalism during the war years, Forster rode out what could have been a totally unproductive and even debilitating period. Instead, he managed to endure the war's horrors while improving his understanding of the East and also fulfilling his own sexual, emotional, and intellectual needs.

During the war years, Cavafy and Forster both shared a determination to avoid being artistically stifled. Cavafy escaped into his world of poesy, a haven where he could fashion historic portraits that offered ironic comments on the present. Forster, in turn, focused his energies on the acute observation of Alexandrian life, the "slow Levantine dégringloade,"[12] as he once put it. His earliest journalistic pieces were written for *The Egyptian Gazette* and *The Egyptian Mail*, a number of which were later republished in *Pharos and Pharillon*, *Abinger Harvest*, and *The Athenaeum*.[13] These essays show Forster's gradual appreciation and comprehension of Cavafy's Levantine world. In "A Musician in Egypt," Forster comments on the artificial nature of Alexandrian "cosmopolitanism" which has always been an equivocal if not problematic quality:

We are exiled here in Egypt for the purpose of doing various little jobs—eggs, cotton, onions, administration and so on—and out of a population of exiled little jobbers it is impossible that a heroic art should be raised. Michelangelo, Shakespeare, Beethoven, Tolstoy—they must in the nature of things spring from a less cosmopolitan society. But what coastal Egypt can do and what from time to time it had done is to produce eclectic artists, who look for their inspiration to Europe. In the days of the Ptolemies they looked to Sicily and Greece, in the days of St. Athanasius to Byzantium, in the 19th century it seemed they would look to France. But there was always this straining of the eyes beyond the sea, always this turning away from Africa, the vast, the formless, the helpless and unhelpful, the pachyderm.[14]

Whether Forster would have included Cavafy in this category of exiles is unclear; but he was quick to respond to the artificiality of a culture which, from its very foundation, had an undeniable colonial dimension.

Forster eventually builds up enough confidence to move beyond the European enclaves of the city into the reality of the indigenous world. This foray was prompted by his romantic relationship with the Egyptian tram conductor Mohammed el Adl, which brought him into increasing contact with the native Arab population. El Adl exerted a strong influence on Forster's Egyptian writings and through him Forster began to see firsthand the poverty and injustice that dominated the lives of the fellahin. Furthermore, his relationship with el Adl was the first sexually fulfilling relationship Forster had ever experienced. Not surprisingly, Forster wrote *Pharos and Pharillon* as a cryptic offering to el Adl, and its Greek dedication to Hermes Psychopompos was undoubtedly a tribute to his memory.[15]

In his letters to Cavafy, Forster continually refers to the process of producing and publishing his Egyptian books, converting what began as journalistic pieces into polished literary essays. The humor and determination they display evince Forster's resilient spirit and unwavering humanism, even during a time of war. Forster would eventually extend his creative energies to Cavafy, who allegedly helped him with his research. In the process, he became increasingly enamored of Cavafy's poetry and intrigued by his personality. The essay on Cavafy that Forster included in *Pharos and Pharillon* still stands as one of the most incisive and eloquent appraisals of Cavafy's poetry and character:

> He may be prevailed upon to begin a sentence—an immense complicated yet shapely sentence, full of parentheses that never get mixed and of reservations that really do reserve; a sentence that moves with logic to its foreseen end, yet to an end that is always more vivid and thrilling than one foresaw. Sometimes the sentence is finished in the street, sometimes the traffic murders it, sometimes it lasts into the flat. It deals with the tricky behaviour of the Emperor Alexius Comnenus in 1096, or with olives, their possibilities and price, or with the fortunes of friends, or George Eliot, or the dialects of the interior of Asia Minor. It is delivered with equal ease in Greek, English, or French. And despite its intellectual richness and human outlook, despite the matured charity of its judgments, one feels that it too stands at a slight angle to the universe: it is the sentence of a poet.[16]

This essay first presented Cavafy to the English speaking world, and its importance and impact cannot be overestimated. Indeed, Forster would later write, "I did a little to spread his fame. It was about the best thing I did."[17] Forster places Cavafy not in the ethereal world of poetry, but squarely within the historical context of Hellenism: "Alexandria, his birthplace, came into being just when Public School Greece decayed; kings, emperors, patriarchs have trodden the ground between his office and his flat; his literary ancestor—if he has one—is Callimachus. . . ."[18] In the later version of the essay, other significant qualities are noted—Cavafy's "amoral mind" and "Mediterranean complexity" among them:

His material as a poet, then, begins with his own experiences and sensations: his interest in courage and cowardice and bodily pleasure, and so on. He begins from within. But he never makes a cult of himself or of what he feels. All the time he is being beckoned to and being called to by history, particularly by the history of his own race. History, too, is full of courage, cowardice, lust, and is to that extent domestic. But it is something more. It is an external inspiration. And he found in the expanses and recesses of the past, in the clash of great names and the tinkle of small ones, in the certified victories and slurred defeats, in the jewels and the wounds and the vast movements beginning out of nothing and sometimes ending nowhere: he found in them something that transcended his local life and freshened and strengthened his art. Demurely, ironically, he looks into the past, for he knew the answers. Cleopatra did not win Actium. Julian did not reinstate paganism. Anna Comnena took the wrong side. The Senate sit in state to receive the barbarians; news comes that there are no barbarians, so the Senate have nothing to do. . . .[19]

To his credit, Forster was one of the first critics to appreciate the unique difference between Cavafy's Hellenism and the received classical tradition:

The civilization he respected was a bastardy in which the Greek strain prevailed, and into which, age after age, outsiders would push, to modify and be modified. If the strain died out—never mind: it had done its work, and it would have left, far away upon some Asian upland, a coin of silver, stamped with the exquisite head of a Hellenizing king. Pericles, Aristides, Themistocles, schoolroom tyrants: what did they know of this extension which is still extending, and which sometimes seemed (while he spoke) to connote the human race?[20]

Even Cavafy's indomitable racial pride is discreetly alluded to in this final sentence. Forster's remarkable insights notwithstanding, it should be noted that although the novelist understood Cavafy's Hellenic world well enough, he himself, as a trained classicist, did not share the poet's view of Hellenism's survival into the Late Antique and Byzantine periods. In fact, these profoundly significant differences regarding the continuity of Hellenism would figure greatly in the course of their future collaboration.

The intensity of Forster's appreciation and interest in Cavafy has given rise to the idea that Cavafy was the sort of poet Forster would have been had he written verse.[21] In fact, an early reviewer of *Pharos and Pharillon* noted:

> In one of its all-too often fragmentary essays, there comes a sudden enchanting glimpse, at an Alexandrian street-corner, of a "gentleman in a straw hat, standing absolutely motionless at a slight angle to the universe." Actually, it is the figure of Mr. C.P. Cavafy, a contemporary Demotic poet of the city, yet somehow—remove the straw hat, and animate (but slightly) that immobility . . . is this not Mr. Forster himself?[22]

Forster himself would have been greatly flattered by this impression and may have even encouraged it. Included in this volume are two unpublished compositions that were clearly attempts (albeit mediocre ones) at Cavafian homo-erotica (see Appendix). The first is titled "That the Mere Glimpse" and was written at Weybridge in 1920 in confessed imitation of Cavafy. The second, "To See a Sinadino Again," sentimentally recalls the men of the Sinadinos family whom he met while living in Alexandria. It becomes clear from such poems that Forster identified artistically with Cavafy and had deeply assimilated his Alexandrian experience. This is relayed by the final couplet of the second poem, where "The thought has blossomed in exquisite flower, / And Alexandria returns for an hour."[23]

Early comparative readings of Forster and Cavafy have taken this imitative enthusiasm as a point of interpretative departure. There is, however, a reverse side to this Alexandrian coin, one that greatly qualifies all the shared enthusiasm and even the common tradition of classical Hellenism out of which both novelist and poet were working. This has to do with a profound discrepancy over the evolution of Alexandrian Hellenism and its assimilation of and absorption into the Oriental word. Forster's approach to Hellenistic Egypt and the Christianity that followed in its wake puts him at odds with Cavafy, contrary to what most comparative readings have claimed. The biting sarcasm and dismissive tone of many of the essays in *Pharos and Pharillon* remove them from the realm of Cavafian ideas. Forster's tone recalls that of Edward Gibbon in *The Decline and Fall of the Roman Empire*, particularly his "dryly malicious accounts of the Church Fathers."[24] This element alone would have troubled Cavafy, whose view of Late Antique and Byzantine culture constituted, in essence, a repudiation of Gibbon. For Cavafy valued the singular role the church fathers played in preserving and disseminating classical Greek education *(paideia)*. Nor would Cavafy have agreed with Forster's reductive view of Alexandrian culture—both ancient and modern—as an artificial European export imposed upon an indigenous population. To Cavafy's mind, there was no clear line separating Greece from the Orient. Nor was the Orient extraneous to Hellenistic culture and the ecumenical Hellenism it produced, but rather it remained an intrinsic and indispensable part of it, as his numerous poems foregrounding the Orient evince.[25]

Forster's Egyptian essays, for all their merits, possess a "jocular condescension," as John Colmer put it,[26] which troubled many readers, particularly Lionel Trilling, who faulted them for their unacceptable "archness" and "lofty whimsicality": "Under Forster's implacable gentleness, the past becomes what it should never be, quaint, harmless and ridiculous."[27] While it is true that these pieces are "no mere belletristic exercises, but attempts to capture the past in order to make ironic comments on the present,"[28] they nevertheless suffer from a certain English smugness and frequently lapse into error—another complication for Cavafy who notoriously obsessed over matters of historical accuracy.[29] The specter of Gibbon hovers notably over Forster's treatment of St. Athanasius in *Pharos and Pharillon*, where the saint is portrayed as a scheming "coadjutor" who, along with his fanatic coreligionists, destroyed Alexandria and its Greek legacy:

> Roused by his [Athanasius'] passage from older visions, the soul
> of the world began to stir, and to what activity! Heavy Romans,
> dreamy Orientals and quick Greeks all turned to theology, and
> scrambled for the machinery of the Pagan State, wrenching this
> way and that until their common heritage was smashed. Cleopatra's
> temple to Antony first felt the killing glare of truth. Arians and
> Orthodox competed for its consecration, and in the space of six
> years its back was broken and its ribs cracked by fire.[30]

A similarly negative spirit animates Forster's essay on St. Clement, whose praiseworthy attempt to fuse Greek *paideia* with Christian doctrine was ultimately in vain:

> Christianity, though she contained little that was fresh doctrinally,
> yet descended with a double-edged sword that hacked the ancient
> world to pieces. For she had declared war against two great
> forces — Sex and the State — and during her complicated contest
> with them the old order was bound to disappear.[31]

Two very problematic issues are raised here — that the old order disappeared with the rise of Christianity, and that Greek culture and the Christian God were incompatible. Neither of these views would have been acceptable to Cavafy. Indeed, Christian Antioch was the setting of many of his erotic poems, and the city where the Emperor Julian the Apostate was ridiculed by the Christian Antiocheans precisely because his paganism was puritanical, whereas their Christianity was a delicate amalgam of pagan licentiousness and new-found piety.[32]

The Forster–Cavafy letters mask ideological discrepancies which become more apparent when approached from an intertextual perspective. Although in his letters to Forster Cavafy compliments *Pharos and Pharillon*, his private views of Forster's handling of these topics (as reflected in his poems) express an altogether different angle. For example, Cavafy began composing an unfinished poem on Saint Athanasius in 1920, when Forster was at the peak of his journalistic activity and publishing his Egyptian essays in *The Athenaeum*. His poem clearly speaks to a different Alexandria and shows, among other things, how incompatible were the Englishman's reformed predisposition toward eastern Christianity and the Alexandrian's own sense of church history:

> In a boat upon the Great Nile,
> accompanied by two fellow monks,
> the fleeing and beleaguered Athanasius
> — the virtuous, the pious, the keeper of the true faith —
> prayed. His enemies had persecuted him
> and he had but little hope of surviving.
> The wind was against them,
> and their rotting vessel sailed with much difficulty.
>
> Upon finishing his prayer
> he turned his mournful face
> to his brothers — and wondered,
> seeing their strange smiles.
> For while he was praying, the monks
> had divined what had happened
> in Mesopotamia; the monks
> knew how that very moment
> the rogue Julian had passed away.[33]

Although the source for this poem was the same one that Forster consulted for his guide (E.L. Butcher's *The Story of the Church in Egypt*), the poem was undoubtedly animated by Cavafy's tacit disapproval of Forster's reductive theory of Hellenism and condescending presentation of the eastern Christian saint. For in the poem, it is clearly Julian who is the malefactor (as he is in so many of Cavafy's poems), whereas Athanasius, "the keeper of the true faith," inspires a divine vision in his fellow monks.

Ironically, it is precisely in the text where we expect to find the most intertextual harmony where we encounter the greatest antiquarian dissonance; for *Alexandria: A History and a Guide* contains some of Forster's most startlingly un-Cavafian pronouncements. Indeed, there are a number of statements in Forster's guide that Cavafy would have found problematic if not utterly preposterous. (Oddly enough, Cavafy refrained from commenting on these myriad discrepancies and what, to his mind, would have been cultural fallacies.) Take, for example, Forster's dismissive assertion that "St. Catherine of Alexandria is also said to have died under Diocletian, but it is improbable that she ever lived: she and her wheel were creations of Western Catholicism, and the land of her supposed sufferings has only recognized her out of politeness to the French."[34] Here one wonders how Forster could ignore the looming presence of the sixth-century monastery on Mount Sinai built by the Emperor Justinian and later rededicated to Saint Catherine? His assertions here certainly minimize the historical importance of this oasis of Byzantine Christianity and slight the significance of the saint's cult in the Levant.

In addition to this historical inaccuracy, there is also the adverse theory of Hellenism's demise that Forster advances as an historical hypothesis. Forster selects the tragic persona of Hypatia to illustrate his thesis: "She is not a great figure. But with her the Greece that is a spirit expired—the Greece that tried to discover truth and create beauty and that had created Alexandria."[35] Forster's Keatsean Greece of truth and beauty remains fundamentally irreconcilable with Cavafy's Hellenic continuum. Even Byzantine Hellenism is dismissed as an oppressive imperial presence:

Now and then an Emperor tried to heal the schism [between the Monophysites and the Orthodox], and made concessions to the Egyptian faith. But the schism was racial, the concessions theological, so nothing was effected. Egypt was only held for the

Empire by Greek garrisons, and consequently when the Arabs came they conquered her at once.[36]

This view of an Egyptian 'nationalist movement' started by Monophysite monks hardly squares with Cavafy's notion of a highly cultured and flexible ecumenical Hellenism that he felt suffused the Near East up until the fall of Byzantium.

Perhaps the most shocking of the book's many discrepancies is Forster's trivializing account of the British bombardment of Alexandria in 1882:

> The bombardment succeeded, though Arabi's gunners in the forts fought bravely. In the evening the Superb blew up the powder magazine in Fort Adda. Fort Kait Bey was also shattered and the minaret of its fifteenth-cent. Mosque was seen "melting away like ice in the sun." The town, on the other hand, was scarcely damaged, as our gunners were careful in their aim.[37]

As we have no record of Cavafy's thoughts on this matter, we cannot but wonder how he might have received this statement, given that the Cavafy residence was destroyed during the raids, as were the homes and businesses of a great many of his friends.[38] In addition to it being an opportunity to level the economic ascendancy of the non-British merchants in the city, the bombardment was an occasion to test out new machine guns and demonstrate Britain's military power.[39] In essence, it was a gratuitous display of imperial brutality.

In commemoration of Cavafy, Forster dedicated the second edition of *Alexandria* (1938) to the poet. In a letter dated 31 December 1922, Forster thanked the poet for his help in both books (see letter 18). Cavafy was duly appreciative of being included in *Pharos and Pharillon*, as may be seen in his letter to Forster dated 10 July 1923 (see letter 21). Cavafy's cordial but laconic response to Forster's magnanimous tribute to him is curious, as is his rather flat acceptance of what, given Cavafy's own poems, clearly would have been unconscionable historical portraits and blatant factual errors. It should be kept in mind that Cavafy's letter was written only months after the catastrophic defeat of the Greek armies in Asia Minor,[40] and it is indeed likely that the poet's mind was preoccupied with more grave matters.

Based on these intertextual examples, it becomes apparent that Cavafy was being less than sincere in his written exchanges with Forster. In addition to not wanting to appear ungrateful to Forster for introducing him to the English-speaking world, Cavafy was undoubtedly unsure about the proper response to Forster and his determination to bring out an English edition of his poems. The "grateful, but very stiff and impersonal, replies" Forster received from Cavafy are quite telling of this ambivalence (Forster himself referred to them as "a mixture here of caution and courtesy").[41] Cavafy's letters to Forster are tainted by the official bureaucratic tone he most likely used when composing letters in his capacity as secretary at the Irrigation Office, where he was responsible for overseeing correspondence (a parodic inversion of the prestigious position of *ab epistulis graecis* held by the Greek sophists in the Roman Empire). Cavafy began his professional life at the Third Circle of Irrigation as a copyist and supervised English-language correspondence. Letter writing was, one could say, his profession. According to his colleague Ibrahim el Kayar, Cavafy "corrected not only our letters but those of other offices. He would correct the same letter many times and insist pedantically on marks of punctuation."[42] Given this epistolary fact, one cannot but appreciate the calculated reserve and Byzantine diplomacy (and even duplicity) of Cavafy's letters to Forster, whose style is almost silly in comparison.[43] Take, for example, Forster's letter of 7 July 1922 signed "Yours Britishly and forever," or his complaint of 11 November 1923: "All mourn, all deplore, / Both Gentile and Jew, / That they hear no more / From you. / Yours inconsolably / Fellow-Poet."

The even more vexing question remains as to why Cavafy, given all of Forster's efforts and auspicious connections—T.S. Eliot, T.E. Lawrence, and Leonard Woolf were enlisted for this publishing project—remained seemingly uninterested. The common explanation offered for Cavafy's lack of expediency and withholding of his official imprimatur is that his translator, George Valassopoulo, tarried with the translations, owing to his disapproval of the erotic poetry.[44] The theory that Cavafy fore-stalled an English edition of his poems so that he could publish one in Greek[45] may have some validity, as has Forster's fanciful view that Cavafy did not complete a volume for the same reason that Pope Julius II did not finish building his tomb.[46] Cavafy was no doubt grateful to Forster for his efforts, and always polite, returning the novelist's sentiments of friendship and praising his novels, particularly *A Passage to India* (see letters 45 and 69). Permission for an authorized publication, however, was never granted, despite Forster's persistence. Amazingly enough, Forster appears not to have been insulted by Cavafy's attitude. In a letter to George Savidis dated 6 January 1964, Forster wrote "It is natural that his [letters] should be the more reserved. He was not as anxious to know me as I him."[47] Certainly Forster knew who the chief saboteur was in all this: "Deep behind it all is Cavafy."[48]

One name which surfaces in the letters and provides an intriguing clue to understanding Cavafy's behavior is that of the historian Arnold Toynbee. Forster records his well-intentioned but problematic decision to involve Toynbee in his translation project. During the early 1920s, the historian's name was anathema to Greeks of both the nation and diaspora since his appointment as the first Koraes Professor of Modern Greek and Byzantine History, Language, and Literature at King's College, London. Toynbee's articles for the *Manchester Guardian*, and the ill-timed publication of his book *The Western Question in Greece and Turkey* (1922), led him to resign from the chair in 1923.[49] Coincidentally, Cavafy himself had been considered as a lecturer for this chair, as Richard Clogg has discovered.[50] Cavafy's connections with Alexandrian Greeks abroad would certainly have kept him abreast of the situation in London. In fact, a number of the donors for the establishment of the chair were relatives of the Cavafy family and former business associates in Manchester and London, namely the Ionides, Cassavetti, and Ralli families.[51]

Toynbee's views on the events in Asia Minor amounted to a scandal for the Greek community. Most objectionable to the donors of the chair were Toynbee's unabashed sympathy for the Turkish resistance and his unsparing account of Greek atrocities against the Turkish populace of Asia Minor. To his credit, Toynbee put the blame for the catastrophe on the West and the politics of "Westernization."[52] This theory, advanced as it was for its time, did little to assuage the outraged sensibilities of Greek politicians and British philhellenes. Particularly apt here are the comments of R.W. Seton-Watson, Masaryk Professor of Central European History at King's College, London: "At the supreme crisis in the fate of the Greek nation—probably without exaggeration the most decisive since Xerxes" Toynbee had "plunged into a violent propagandist campaign in favour of the Turks."[53] Toynbee's journalistic role and attempts to influence British policy in the Near East[54] were certainly known to Cavafy, and could not but have had a negative influence on his dealings with Forster. The poet was most likely reluctant to enter the circle of literati into which Forster seemed intent on bringing him. It is most alarming to note Forster's lack of discretion where the personality of Toynbee was concerned.[55] And it is quite possible that Cavafy had read Forster's own pro-Turkish articles and was chary of being associated with him and his group of Turkish sympathizers, especially since his reputation as a poet was far from established in Greece.

The politics of empire provides one lens through which to read the Forster–Cavafy letters; the business of publishing and translating offers yet another. Forster's determination to bring Cavafy before the English reading public resulted in the poet's association—in print at least—with some of the most significant names in modernist literature. This is a dimension of Forster's efforts that can only be fully appreciated by perusing the contents of the journals in which Cavafy was published, examples of which have been reproduced as plates in this volume. In *The Oxford Outlook*, for instance, Cavafy's name appears with Graham Greene, Cecil Day-Lewis, and Robert Graves (see letter 31). In *The Chapbook*, he joins Leonard Woolf, Conrad Aiken, H.D., Wyndham Lewis, Jean Cocteau, and Aldous Huxley (see letter 49). In *The Criterion*, he is featured along with Marcel Proust, W.B. Yeats, Virginia Woolf, and Hugh Walpole. And had he published during his lifetime with the Hogarth Press, his poetry volume would have appeared alongside the writings of T.S. Eliot, Sigmund Freud, and Virginia Woolf, works which, as S.P. Rosenbaum notes, "were the most outstanding contributions of the Hogarth Press to modern culture."[56]

The inclusion of seventeen letters from Forster to George Valassopoulo was deemed necessary to balance out the epistolary narrative; they chart the outcome of the ill-fated anthology that Forster, Valassopoulo, and Cavafy were working toward producing. A complex story unfolds here: the initial plan for a volume of twenty-five poems with the Hogarth Press in 1923 (see letter 29) never materialized owing to delays and a lack of agreement on the selection of historic versus erotic poems; and a subsequent scheme for a volume of the historical poems is scuttled by Leonard Woolf's decision (authorized by Cavafy's heir, Alekos Singopoulo) to publish John Mavrogordato's translations of the complete poems.[57] During the course of events, Forster becomes increasingly entangled in a contest between Valassopoulo and Mavrogordato over securing authorization for the first volume of translated poems. Forster's final contribution to this project was to have been an introduction to the Hogarth Press volume, which, as it turned out, was penned instead by Rex Warner in 1949 owing to Forster's procrastination. (In early 1949, before approaching Warner, Woolf had asked T.S. Eliot to write the introduction; Eliot, who had just received the Nobel prize for literature in 1948, declined.) Although we do not know specifically why Forster withheld what would have been the crowning culmination of his Cavafy project (his behavior oddly mirrors Cavafy's refusal to authorize Forster to act as his agent), we may safely surmise that his sense of loyalty to Valassopoulo and private reservations about the quality of Mavrogordato's translations (see letters 84 and 86) were among the chief reasons.[58] (It should be noted that a similar debacle over the authorization of the first official French edition ensued in 1947, with Alekos Singopoulo rejecting the translation of Marie-Jeanne Colombe in preference for an edition by George

Papoutsakis.)[59] Certainly Forster felt some degree of remorse over not standing by Valassopoulo in 1944 when he might have exerted some influence on both Woolf and Singopoulo. Forster's letter to Valassopoulo in 1955 (letter 84), where he relays how he shares his students' preference for Valassopoulo's over Mavrogordato's translations, speaks volumes about his regrets and lingering loyalty to his fellow Kingsman.

The letters conclude, as they commence, with a note addressed by Forster to a fellow Kingsman named George—the late George Savidis, the doyen of Cavafy studies to whom the meticulous preservation of these letters and documentation of related archival materials may be credited. In a letter to Savidis dated 13 May 1949, Forster expressed his desire to show him the "Cavafy stuff." Some years later in 1964, Savidis sent Forster copies of Cavafy's drafts along with copies of Forster's surviving letters, thus rekindling the intimacy between the two and setting the stage for the eventual publication of the surviving material.[60] It is during these late exchanges with Savidis that Forster gives us his most candid assessments of the relationship—how Cavafy remained somewhat aloof, that he was behind the Byzantine machinations delaying the translation project, and that "it was not until my last Egyptian visit that we spoke simply and naturally. I am always so happy that this was achieved."[61] We also have Forster's proud admission that meeting and promoting Cavafy was "one of my triumphs," a most fitting concluding comment on the entire project (see letter 86).

In closing, a few words on the Valassopoulo anthology are in order. The fate of the Valassopoulo translations is a parallel narrative, the full story of which deserves a separate comprehensive study. The forty-six poems gathered for this anthology constitute all extant Valassopoulo translations to date. In letters exchanged between Valassopoulo and Cavafy in 1925, Valassopoulo mentions forty-six poems that were in the process of being polished. If we add to this number the five missing poems that are mentioned in the letters,[62] then we end up with a total of fifty-one poems which, we may safely conclude, constituted the prospective corpus of fifty poems selected by Valassopoulo for his intended volume. The poems included in the present anthology mark the first publication of Valassopoulo's work in full; they are presented as a belated tribute to his selfless work and unique appreciation and transmission of Cavafy's voice and art.

The texts of the poems are transcriptions of the final typescripts as they exist in either the Cavafy Archive in Athens or the Forster Archive at King's College, with minor editorial adjustments and corrections.[63] Although an edition of the poems documenting all the various emendations and identifying the specific contributions of Forster, Valassopoulo, and Cavafy (along with those of Felix de Menasce, Arnold Toynbee, Robert Furness, and T.E. Lawrence) is not possible given the incomplete state of the surviving manuscripts, future discoveries might uncover notebooks and earlier drafts that could generate a full scholarly edition. In their present state, the poems were 'polished' by different hands and at various stages in the triangulated collaboration. With the exception of the translations done by Cavafy's brother John[64] and the few poems translated by Christopher Scaife,[65] these texts comprise the only English translations possessing Cavafy's imprimatur and thus they are of singular value to the history of his poetry in translation. It is hoped that they will provide their readership with a fitting corollary to the letters and make for a complete and satisfying experience in and of themselves.

Translation, as Walter Benjamin famously wrote, is the "afterlife of a work of art"; letters, one might add, are the afterlife of the labor of friendship. In the case of Forster and Cavafy, translations and letters intersect at the site of art and friendship; as such, their letters and poems have been presented, annotated, and transcribed with a view to reconstructing the fascinating historical events and personal affections that generated them. More importantly, they have been contextualized within the array of personalities and literary currents which readers will require to fully appreciate them. It is hoped that the publication of the Forster–Cavafy correspondence will make a significant contribution to the history of modernism and illuminate a literary friendship from new angles both slight and great.

Notes

Abbreviations Used in the Notes

Allott   E.M. Forster. *Alexandria and Pharos and Pharillon*, ed. Miriam Allott. London: Andre Deutsch, 2004.

Haag   Michael Haag. *Alexandria: City of Memory*. New Haven: Yale University Press, 2004; Cairo: The American University in Cairo Press, 2004.

Letters   Mary Lago and P.N. Furbank, eds. *Selected Letters of E.M. Forster*. 2 vols. Cambridge: Belknap Press, 1983.

Liddell   Robert Liddell. *Cavafy: A Biography*. 2nd ed. London: Duckworth, 2000.

Life   P.N. Furbank. *E.M. Forster: A Life*. 2 vols. New York: Harcourt Brace Jovanovich, 1977, 1978.

* An asterisk indicates a title translated from the Greek.

1   *Letters*, vol. 1, xi–xii. Furbank notes that Forster's letters to Cavafy show him in a most attractive light (xi).

2   See Dimitris Daskalopoulos' essay "C.P. Cavafy as a Correspondent*" in *On the Outskirts of Antioch and Keryneia: Cavafy—Seferis** (Athens: Ikaros, 2006), 70–89, where he comments on how Cavafy's letters share similar aesthetic qualities with his poems, notably a limited but carefully chosen vocabulary expressed in a reserved style (78).

3   Only two actual letters sent by Cavafy to Forster survive, one dated 1 August 1924 and the other 15 October 1929.

4   On Cavafy's fear of the finality of print, see Liddell, 141.

5   Forster conducted an extensive purging of letters when he moved out of West Hackhurst in 1946 (*Letters*, vol. 1, xvii).

6   On these mutual influences, see Jane Lagoudis Pinchin, *Alexandria Still* (Princeton: Princeton University Press, 1977), George Savidis, "Cavafy and Forster" in *Small Cavafy Pieces A** (Athens: Hermes, 1985), 169–78, and Peter Jeffreys, *Eastern Questions: Hellenism and Orientalism in the Writings of E.M. Forster and C.P. Cavafy* (Greensboro: ELT Press, 2005), chap. 1 and passim.

7   Others claim the introduction was effected by George Antonius and Pericles Anastasiades. See Haag, 28 and passim, and Dimitris Daskalopoulos, *The Life and Work of C.P. Cavafy** (Athens: Metaichmio, 2001), 78.

8   As W.H. Auden wrote, "What, then, is it that survives translation and excites? Something I can only call, most inadequately, a tone of voice, a personal speech. I have read translations of Cavafy made by many different hands, but every one of them was immediately recognizable as a poem by Cavafy; nobody else could possibly have written it." W.H. Auden, "Introduction" to

The Complete Poems of Cavafy, trans. Rae Dalven (New York: Harcourt Brace and Co., 1989), xvi.

9   See Alexander Kitroeff, *The Greeks in Egypt* (London: Ithaca Press, 1989) and Timothy Mitchell, *Colonising Egypt* (Berkeley: University of California Press, 1991).

10 Wilfred Stone, *The Cave and the Mountain* (Stanford: Stanford University Press, 1966), 282, 286.

11 *Letters*, vol. 1, 238–39.

12 This peculiar term connotes a rapid deterioration, decadence, and a change from bad to worse, all of which meanings apply to Forster's initially negative response to Egypt.

13 For an overview of the composition of these essays, see Hilda Spear, ed., *The Uncollected Egyptian Essays of E.M. Forster* (Blackness Press, 1988), 7. A number of these essays also appear in *The Prince's Tale and Other Uncollected Writings*, ed. P.N. Furbank (London: Penguin Books, 1998). For recent appreciations and critiques of these texts, see David Cowart, "Where Sense Verges into Spirit: E.M. Forster's *Alexandria* after 75 Years" in *Michigan Quarterly Review* 36.3 (1997): 484–93, where he argues that Forster's guide exhibits an "uncanny anticipation" of "postcolonial perspectives" (484). See also Miriam Allott's excellent "Editor's Introduction" to the Abinger Edition (vol. 16) of *Alexandria and Pharos and Pharillon* (Allott, xv–lxxi).

14 Spear, *The Uncollected Egyptian Essays of E.M. Forster*, 39. For two radically different approaches to Alexandria's cosmopolitanism, see Michael Haag's *Vintage Alexandria: Photographs of the City, 1860–1960* (Cairo: The American University in Cairo Press, 2008) and Hala Halim, "Forster in Alexandria: Gender and Genre in Narrating Colonial Cosmopolitanism," in *Hawwa* 4.2–3 (2006): 237–73.

15 Judith Scherer Herz, "The Remaking of the Past in Forster's Non-Fiction" in *Twentieth Century Literature* 31.2–3 (1985): 287–96, 291.

16 Allott, 245.

17 From a brief essay, "C.P. Cavafy: 1863–1933" published in the *Umbrella* (1958), 5.

18 Allott, 247.

19 E.M. Forster, "The Complete Poems of C.P. Cavafy" in *Two Cheers for Democracy*, Abinger Edition, vol. 11, ed. Oliver Stallybrass (London: Edward Arnold, 1972), 233, 237, 235–36.

20 Ibid., 237. For a critique of Cavafy's elitist attitude towards indigenous Egyptian culture, see Khaled Fahmy, "For Cavafy, with Love and Squalor" in *Alexandria Real and Imagined,* ed. Anthony Hirst (Aldershot: Ashgate, 2004), 263–79, who writes "Nor is Cavafy's poetry so remote from the discourse of cosmopolitanism, despite numerous references to what one must

assume were Arabic-speak locals. . . . Only minimally does he belong to the Alexandria he lived in or to the real people who inhabited it" (273–74).

21 See Nicola Beauman, *E.M. Forster: A Biography* (New York: Alfred Knopf, 1994), 297, and Pinchin, *Alexandria Still*, 125 and passim.

22 Philip Gardner, ed., *E.M. Forster: The Critical Heritage* (London: Routledge and Kegan Paul, 1973), 194.

23 Both poems were recently published in *The Creator as Critic and Other Writings by E.M. Forster*, ed. Jeffrey M. Heath (Toronto: Dundum Press, 2008), 731, 734.

24 Stone, *The Cave*, 285. Allott also notes that "Forster as a historian was always closer to Gibbon than Cavafy" (Allott, xlix).

25 See Jeffreys, *Eastern Questions*, chap. 4 and passim.

26 John Colmer, *E.M. Forster: The Personal Voice* (London: Routledge and Kegan Paul, 1975), 144.

27 Lionel Trilling, *E.M. Forster* (New York: New Directions, 1964), 138–39.

28 Stone, *The Cave*, 284–85.

29 Forster's errata brought Robert Tracey to write in his review, "Nor is it of much value as a history of Alexandria since it is full of blunders of one sort or another . . . many of these mistakes are minor ones, but taken altogether they add up to a book which has . . . an error on every fourth or fifth page. . . . If he is weak on history, his theology is even weaker, a serious problem in a book whose core is an account of the 'spiritual city' of Alexandria" (Allott, 382–83). On Cavafy's penchant for historical accuracy, see Liddell, 123–24.

30 Allott, 217. The essay was first published in August 1918 in *The Egyptian Mail* and later in *The Athenaeum* in May 1919 (Allott, 311).

31 Ibid., 213.

32 See Glen Bowersock, "The Julian Poems of C.P. Cavafy" in *Byzantine and Modern Greek Studies*, vol. 7 (1981): 89–104, where he writes that Antioch "was a profoundly important symbol for him: its people were immoral . . . but their life was delectable. . . . And they were Christian. They were also Greek. . . . Permissive Christianity, then, appears to be the fundamental interest of Cavafy in handling the various Julian episodes. To be a Christian did not preclude being a pagan in the old sense . . ." (102–103).

33 My translation, *C.P. Cavafy: The Unfinished Poems**, ed. Renata Lavagnini (Athens: Ikaros, 1994), 106. Cavafy's poem is literally a poetic transposition of E.L. Butcher's prose.

34 Allott, 48. This erroneous information was taken from E.L. Butcher, *The Story of the Church of Egypt*, vol. 1, (London: Smith, Elder, and Co., 1897), 125, who dismissively equates Saint Catherine with Sitte Dimiana, regarding whom, see Aziz Atiya, ed., et al., *The Coptic Encyclopedia*, vol. 3 (New York: Maxwell MacMillan International, 1991), 903. The Monastery of Saint Catherine on Mount Sinai took the name of the saint after acquiring

her relics in the tenth or eleventh century, independent of any western traditions. See the *Oxford Dictionary of Byzantium*, vol. 2, ed. Alexander Kazhdan (New York: Oxford University Press, 1991), 392. Her cult in the West was "born and developed in Normandy, Flanders, and the Rhineland, where monks from Sinai came to beg for their monastery, soon bringing relics of the saint" (Atiya, vol. 5, 1976).

35 Allott, 51.

36 Ibid., 52. This theory, which Forster gleaned from Samuel Sharpe's *The History of Egypt* (1885) and E.L. Butcher's *The Story of the Church of Egypt* (1897), has been challenged by G.W. Bowersock in his *Hellenism in Late Antiquity* (Ann Arbor: University of Michigan Press, 1990), and Roger S. Bagnall, *Egypt in Late Antiquity* (Princeton: Princeton University Press, 1993).

37 Allott, 80.

38 Upon orders from the British consulate, the Cavafy family fled Alexandria before the bombardment and relocated to Constantinople, a move which caused great hardship and distress. As Liddell notes, the bombardment "left the town in shambles" (31). See Stratis Tsirkas, *Cavafy and his Era**, 2nd ed. (Athens: Kedros, 1971), 93–119, for an account of the disastrous consequences of the bombardment on the Greek community, and chapters 7–9 for a thorough review of the Anglo-Greek political and economic rivalry in Egypt.

39 See Timothy Mitchell, *Colonising Egypt*, 128–29 and passim.

40 The Asia Minor Catastrophe refers to the defeat of the Greek army in Anatolia in August of 1922. The ensuing compulsory exchange of Greek and Turkish populations resulted in the uprooting of 1.5 million Ottoman Greeks, effectively ending the Greek presence in Asia Minor.

41 *Life*, vol. 2, 115 and Savidis, *Small Cavafy Pieces A**, 169. See note 60.

42 Liddell, 127.

43 Cavafy's indifference to Forster's project becomes even more apparent when compared to his enthusiastic response to Mario Vaianos, Forster's Athenian equivalent in matters of publication. Vaianos was a university student whom Cavafy had never met and whose connections in the Athenian literary world allowed him to bring Cavafy to the attention of Greek literati. Cavafy's numerous letters to him (over forty-three) are replete with directives and numerous poems for publication and dissemination. See Cavafy's *Letters to Marios Vaianos**, ed. E.N. Moschos (Athens: Hestia, 1979).

44 Liddell, 185. Cavafy recorded some practical reservations regarding the terms of the contract he received from the Hogarth Press in 1925, which included concerns over the readiness and selection of the poems, unlimited copyright of future editions of the work, Forster's preface and intervention, and foreign language editions (Cavafy Archive).

45 Ibid., 185.

46 E.M. Forster, "Unfinished Talk on Cavafy (1956)," in *The Creator as Critic*, 133.

47 Savidis, 172.

48 In a letter to William Plomer dated 2 July 1945, in which he recounts the problems related to the Valassopoulo–Mavrogordato conflict, Forster expresses his love for Cavafy as the justification for all his prolonged efforts on the poet's behalf, despite the seemingly unending complications (*Letters*, vol. 2, 46). Forster's sentence ("Deep behind it all is Cavafy, whom I loved, and what is best done for his immortality.") indirectly alludes to Cavafy's obstructionism which had an ongoing effect on the fate of the translation project. See Forster's comment on Cavafy's "continued silence" in letter 34.

49 For a full account of this imbroglio, see Richard Clogg, "Politics and the Academy: Arnold Toynbee and the Koraes Chair" in *Middle Eastern Studies*, vol. 21.4 (1985): 1–117.

50 "One of the most interesting proposals for the lectureship in Modern Greek to emerge from [Ronald] Burrow's [Principal of King's College] soundings among Greek friends and acquaintances came from Leon Maccas, the Greek diplomat and director of *Les Etudes Franco-Grecques*. In a letter to Burrows of 28 July 1918, Maccas put forward, among other possible candidates, a Greek man of letters '*de l'école d'Alexandrie . . . qui est un esprit remarquable': a Monsieur Cavafis . . .*" (Clogg 1985: 24).

51 Ibid., 2, 12, 51.

52 In *The Western Question in Greece and Turkey* (London: Constable and Company Ltd., 1923), Toynbee writes, "Neither the Greeks nor the Turks realized the narrowness of the means allowed to the French and British Governments by their public for carrying out policies in the East, and hence they did not perceive that these backers of theirs valued their services only in so far as they relieved them from making efforts themselves. They did not suspect how quickly pawns in distress become an embarrassment, or how little the players care if they disappear from the board. . . . The break-down of Near and of Middle Eastern civilization, the introduction of the Western idea of political nationality, the traditional rivalries of the Powers and the attraction of Greece and Turkey into the vicious cycle, remote though they may have seemed, are the necessary prologue to the Anatolian drama" (100, 108).

53 Clogg 1985: 91. Forster had become a staunch supporter of the Khilafat campaign, the movement in India which condemned British aggression against the Turks and sought to bolster the Ottoman Sultanate. Forster's direct views on the Khilafat movement are expressed in his essay "India and the Turk," which appeared in *The Nation & the Athenaeum* of 30 September 1922. Forster writes that "We may argue that the Khilafat agitation was factitious in its origin and is historically incorrect; but it is not factitious now, it is intertwined deep with his [the Indian Muslim's] faith. He believes that

under God's will the guardianship of Holy Places has passed to the Turks, and that Constantinople itself has become half-holy" (845). David Roessel notes that "Forster knew of the Greek hopes concerning Constantinople . . . from the Greeks he met in Alexandria . . . . Forster did not come around enough to consider their 'Hellenic and Byzantine dreams' anything but warped, even thought the Muslim dreams of the Pan-Islamists at Aligarh were no less so." See David Roessel, "Live Orientals and Dead Greeks: Forster's Response to the Chanak Crisis" in *Twentieth Century Literature*, vol. 36 (1990): 43–60, 55.

54 "Moreover, Toynbee, in addition to his journalistic and other writings on the Greek-Turkish imbroglio, took a more active role in actually trying to shape the course of events, although this was presumably not publicly known at the time. In July 1921, for instance, he sent Forbes Adam of the Foreign Office a summary of a three-hour discussion between himself and Rauf Ahmet Bey, who had accompanied Bekir Sami Bey to the London Conference of February–March of that year at which solution to the crisis had been unsuccessfully sought" (Clogg 1985: 57). Recent archival research by Richard Clogg has uncovered the extent of Toynbee's "mishellenism"—"not merely a dislike of but a profound loathing for the modern Greek." See Clogg's "Beware the Greeks: How Arnold Toynbee Became a Mishellene" in the *Times Literary Supplement* 17 March (2002): 14.

55 Although in his letter to T.S. Eliot of 11 March 1924 (see letter 33), Forster claims that he did not know Toynbee personally, the press coverage of the Koraes debacle was intense, particularly as Toynbee himself went public by publishing his letter of resignation in *The Times* of 3 January 1924. For the full text of this letter, see Clogg 1985: 116–17.

56 See S.P. Rosenbaum, "Leonard and Virginia Woolf at the Hogarth Press" in *Aspects of Bloomsbury: Studies in Modern English Literary and Intellectual History* (New York: St. Martin's Press, 1998), 142–205, 146.

57 In a letter to Forster in 1944, Singopoulo attempts to promote two separate translations or some sort of collaboration between Valassopoulo and Mavrogordato (see note 58). Similarly, Woolf had suggested in 1923 that Cavafy find another translator in England to expedite the publishing process (see letter 29). Presumably, Toynbee could have been enlisted for this task, as Forster hints to Eliot in his letter dated 11 March 1924 (see letter 33). As it turned out, the Mavrogordato edition (1951) took years to be finalized owing to a combination of deterring factors: the war, protracted negotiations with Singopoulo over financial arrangements, and Forster's delay with the introduction.

58 In fairness to Forster, he was in fact traveling throughout North America in 1946 (between April and July) and again between May and June of 1947. The details of the agreement between Woolf and Singopoulo regarding the

Hogarth Press volume are as follows: In 1946, Woolf agrees to publish the complete poems translated by Mavrogordato, with Singopoulo's consent. Singopoulo sends Hogarth Press a cheque for £50 in October 1946 to cover publishing costs. A final contract between Singopoulo and the Hogarth Press is signed on 7 November 1946. The project is delayed, however, due to Forster's tarrying with the introduction. Both Woolf and Singopoulo agree to wait for Forster's essay. Woolf admits to Singopoulo in a letter dated 15 October 1948 that Forster is a "slow writer" but that they should be patient, as the inclusion of his introduction is important (Unpublished Letter, Cavafy Archive). After a delay of four years, the volume goes to press in 1950 (with an introduction by Rex Warner) and is released in 1951.

Prior to this chain of events, Singopoulo had entertained a notion of allowing Valassopoulo to publish an edition of the historical poems in tandem with the Mavrogordato edition (see letters 80 and 81). In a letter written in French dated 11 January 1944, Singopoulo asks Forster to try to reconcile the interests of both editions. Forster is clearly vexed by Singopoulo's plan, which puts him in a difficult position with both translators. Singopoulo abruptly changes his mind and retracts his offer to Valassopoulo. In a letter to Woolf dated 20 June 1946, Singopoulo writes that Valassopoulo's project "would have to be left in abeyance until the moment for the translation and publication of Mr. Cavafy's entire collection would have come out" (Singopoulo File, Cavafy Archive, Athens). In a letter to Forster dated 29 September 1944, Singopoulo apologizes for putting Forster in a difficult position and asks Forster to consider the Valassopoulo project null and void (Singopoulo File, Cavafy Archive). It would appear that Forster's decision to refrain from writing his introduction was deliberate (he could easily have adapted his essay on Cavafy in a relatively brief period of time) and has much to do with the slight to Valassopoulo and the muddle created by Singopoulo.

59 The debacle received wide press coverage and common opinion ran in favor of Colombe and against Singopoulo.

60 In a letter to George Savidis dated 6 January 1964, Forster thanks him for sending the copied correspondence: "The letters excite me most naturally. . . . My own letters interest me most and are certainly easiest to decipher. His are drafts of course—a mixture here of caution and courtesy probably" (Unpublished Letter, King's College, Cambridge).

61 Forster expressed this in a letter to Savidis dated 6 January 1964. See previous note.

62 The missing poems are "Aimilianos Monaí, Alexandrian, A.D. 628–655," "From the School of the Famous Philosopher," "A Byzantine Grandee, in Exile, Composing Verses," "Footsteps," and "Che Fece . . . Il Gran Rifiuto."

In a letter to Valassopoulo dated 29 January 1925, Cavafy asks him about the status of the forty-six poems sent to Forster. The number of poems in Forster's possession, which comprise the collection of typescripts deposited at King's College, totals twenty-four, which indicates that Valassopoulo was aiming for a selection of twenty-five poems, the number discussed for the initial project with Hogarth Press in 1925 (see letter 47) and, alternatively, a collection of fifty poems for a more inclusive volume of the historical poems. It should be noted that not all of the extant poems are strictly historical in nature. Valassopoulo's decision to focus on translating the historical poems was most likely made subsequent to the involvement of Mavrogordato in the translation endeavor.

63 The minor editing includes the restoration of Cavafy's original stanza and line breaks and the elimination of capital letters which were introduced during the various printings of the poems. The editing of the poems from the Cavafy Archive incorporates Cavafy's handwritten emendations to the final drafts and typescripts.

64 John's translations, *Poems by C.P. Cavafy*, were published by Ikaros Press (Athens, 2003). Curiously enough, John submitted his own translations of his brother's poems to *The Athenaeum* in 1919. A letter from the editor (John Middleton Murry) rejected them on the grounds that they were the same poems that had already appeared in *The Athenaeum* in versions by Valassopoulo. This strange episode raises the intriguing question of whether Cavafy knew of or encouraged his brother's effort to compete with Valassopoulo.

65 While living in Egypt, Christopher Scaife collaborated with Cavafy between 1930 and 1932 on the translation of poems that included "The Hall Mirror" (published in *The Spectator* in 1935) and "Myres, Alexandria 340 A.D." See letter 61 for Forster's introduction of Scaife to Cavafy.

The Forster–Cavafy
Letters

1

SULTAN HUSSEIN CLUB[1]

ALEXANDRIA,

EGYPT.

8/10/16

Dear Valassopoulo[2]

Can you dine with me say here on ~~Thurs~~ Wednesday say at 8.15? You will gather I'm open to alternatives. I do hope you can come.

Yours sincerely
EM Forster.

I'm generally at Tel. 2114 from 12-30 to 1-0 and 6-30 to 7-0. And at other hours they'll take a message.

2

SULTAN HUSSEIN CLUB

ALEXANDRIA,

EGYPT.

2 – 1 – ~~16~~ 17

Dear Valassopoulo

It is my unalterable intention to read out aloud to you my unfinished novel on India,[3] and I feel you will be obliged to listen more attentively if you are my guest at dinner first. So will you come and eat the beastly food

---

1   The Sultan Hussein Club, formerly the Khédivial Club, was located at 2 Rue Chérif Pasha on the first floor of the Bourse, which housed Alexandria's cotton and stock exchanges.

2   George Valassopoulo (1890–1972) was Forster's fellow alumnus of King's College, Cambridge, and a lawyer by profession. His family resided in the grand Villa Zancarol in Rue des Fatimites, the so-called Quartier Grec. See plates 8 and 9.

3   *A Passage to India.*

here on Friday at 8.0., after which ~~you~~ we probably repair to Antonius'[4] bedroom.

Thank you for ~~my~~ the note – I got it too late to arrange anything (By the way I'm not Lt.[5] or anything – I like titles but they might make a letter go wrong).

I tried to get you by telephone today.

> Yours ever
> EM Forster.

3

Sultan Hussein Club

Alexandria,
Egypt.

12.5.17

Dear Cavaffy [sic][6]

I think I will herald my resurrection by a letter. Expect me in a few days.

For weeks and weeks I have been, always alternately and sometimes conjointly, too stupid and too lazy to come. But I have often thought of you. Am well.

> Yours ever,
> EM Forster.

---

4   George Antonius (1891–1941), a fellow alumnus of King's College, Cambridge, worked at the Censorship Department in Alexandria during the war. His book, *The Arab Awakening* (1939), played an important role in the emergence of Middle Eastern studies.
5   Forster, as a voluntary worker, had "officer status" (*Life II*, 22).
6   This is the earliest extant letter exchanged between Forster and Cavafy, who met on 7 March 1916 at the Mohammed Ali Club. The rather exuberant tone here and allusion to a "resurrection" is likely connected to Forster's recent acquaintance with Mohammed el Adl, an Egyptian tram conductor with whom he had his first full-fledged romantic relationship.

4

BRITISH RED CROSS CONVALESCENT
HOSPITAL Nº 7
MONTAZAH[7]
ALEXANDRIA.

1.7.17

Dear Cavaffy [sic]

Valassopoulo was over this afternoon and told me that since I saw you something occurred that has made you very unhappy; that you believed the artist must be depraved;[8] and that you were willing he should tell the above to your friends. It made me want to write to you at once, though I gathered nothing clear from him and consequently do not know what to say.

Of late I have been happier than usual myself, and have accepted my good luck with thankfulness and without reservation. But I suspect that at the bottom of one's soul one craves not happiness but peace. I seem to see this when the tide is flowing strongly neither way—I mean when I am disturbed by no great predominance of either joy or sorrow. I don't write this to console you—consolation is a very inferior article which can only be exchanged between people who are not being quite straight with one another. Only there does seem something fundamental in man that is unhappy perhaps, but not with these surface unhappinesses, and that finds its repose not in fruition but in creation. The peace that passeth all understanding is the peace at the heart of a storm. In other words—in extremely other words!—you will go on writing, I believe.

V. and I discussed depravity a little, but not to much effect. He seemed to connect it with passion to which it is (for me) the absolute antithesis. I am not even sure that I connect it with curiosity even, though if it is exists at all it exists as something <u>cold</u>—and would consequently not be a

---

7   The Hospital at Montazah, housed in the former country palace of the ex-Khedive Abbas II, was a grand complex surrounded by lush imperial gardens.

8   Cavafy's view of "depravity" is clarified by direct comments he recorded on the subject: "I'm not sure if perversion gives one strength. Sometimes I think so. But it is certainly the source of greatness." See C.P. Cavafy, *Unpublished Notes on Poetics and Ethics* [in Greek], ed. George Savidis (Athens: Hermes, 1983), 29.

particularly useful ingredient to the artist. That is the only thing I can tell you about depravity—its temperature. No̶ It has nothing to do with material. No action, no thought, is per se depraved.

These two paragraphs are very muddle headed and I shall hardly clear them by telling you that in each I have thought of Dante:[9] first of his remark that the Herald Angels promised not happiness but peace; secondly of the centre of his Hell, which was ice, not fire.

I came here for a couple of days, but as there is work, and the Matron[10] kindly urges me, am stopping on. I shall come and see you as soon as I return. This letter doesn't—then or now—expect an answer. It is only to remind you that among your many friends you have one on the edge of your life in me.

EM Forster

5

SULTAN HUSSEIN CLUB   ALEXANDRIA,
                                                          EGYPT.

10.8.17

My dear George [Valassopoulo]—if I may so say:—
    It seems impossible I should get round on Sunday to improve your

---

9   Forster is alluding to the frozen lake of Cocytus (*The Inferno*, Canto 34). Dante was a favorite subject on which Forster frequently lectured. See his essay/lecture "Dante" (1907), where he quotes from Dante's *The Empire*: "When the shepherds watched their flocks by night, they heard not of riches, nor pleasure, nor honour, nor wealth, nor strength, nor beauty; but of peace; for the celestial soldiery proclaimed Glory to God in the highest, and on earth Peace and Goodwill towards men." See E.M. Forster, *Albergo Empedocle and Other Writings*, ed. George Thomson (New York: Liveright, 1971), 158–59.
10   A reference to Lorna Beatrice Wood, a nurse at the Montazah Convalescent Hospital, where Forster visited, comforted, and occasionally lectured the wounded British soldiers. He also organized classical concerts for the hospital staff and patients.

piano, for Miss Grant Duff[11] has gone to Hospital and Miss Penfold[12] goes swing in the head. I'm so sorry. Let's dine again soon one evening.

I enjoyed that concert so much.

Yours ever

EM Forster.

6

Harnham   Monument Green   Weybridge[13]   18 – 4 – 19

Dear George

You must be thinking me damned ungrateful—I have never answered your letter or thanked you for the very beautiful translations you sent me. But I am not as ungrateful as you think, for I have written our article[14] and arranged for it to come out in the Athenaeum—the most suitable paper in the present state of the press. They only let us have 1500 words, but it's better than nothing, and the right people will read it. I don't know when it comes out. I'll send you a copy of course—also your half of the cheque—also a copy to Cavafy.

I showed <u>The God abandons Antony</u> to Sturge Moore.[15] He much liked it and the translation, only criticising 'your fortune that <u>gives way</u>', which bothered us, you may remember, so I have changed gives way into <u>subsides</u> though I don't like that either.

---

11 Victoria Grant Duff was the head of the Wounded and Missing Department of the Red Cross. As a searcher, Forster reported to Miss Duff, but after being promoted, his relationship with her became strained, and she refused to speak to him (*Life II*, 42).

12 Most likely a relative of Arthur Penfold, who would later review *Alexandria: A History and a Guide* for the *Egyptian Gazette* in 1938/39 (Allott, 377).

13 Forster lived in Weybridge, Surrey, from 1904 to 1925 (see plate 11). He and his mother renamed the house at 19 Monument Green "Harnham" after purchasing it for £1, 075. See Jacqueline Banerjee, *Literary Surrey* (Hampshire: Headley Down, 2007), 157–73.

14 "The Poetry of C.P. Cavafy" was published in *The Athenaeum* on 25 April 1919.

15 Thomas Sturge Moore (1870–1944) was a poet and wood engraver who served as a member of the prestigious Academic Committee of the Royal Society of Literature.

I should be very glad of further translations should you have time —
not only because of the pleasure they ~~have~~ give me but because I have
fallen deeper into journalism & literature than I quite expected (or indeed
intended), and ~~than~~ may find an opportunity of placing them, which
would mean a few piastres for our poet. — Don't hold out hopes to him of
this, though: we must first see how the article goes down.

Today is Good Friday (Western Church). Do you remember what happened last Good Friday? I do. I spent a most pleasant evening at your
house, and ate at dinner (among other things) the most delicious pork
cutlet I have ever tasted: at this lapse of time I may refer to it without
indelicacy I hope.

Rosetta is of course now out of the question — I wrote to Mann[16]
before I had news of the troubles in Egypt[17] asking him to get into touch
with you: under the circumstances he probably has not. I do hope that
all of you have been safe. People here on the whole take little interest
in Egypt, but then they don't take much interest in anything — they are
suffering from overstrain and overwork, and their tempers are abomi-
nable. Perhaps the warmer weather will make a little difference — it
already has to me. I have had 3 weeks holiday in Dorsetshire (where I
saw something of T. Hardy)[18] and now am struggling to review masses
of books — they pour in by every post[19] — I don't think I can stand it for
long, and also it impedes the progress of my own book. Mann has never
once written to me since I left — Thanks for telling Warthan: an 'Early

---

16 Mr. Mann was the editor of Whitehouse Morris, which published Forster's
   Alexandria.
17 In March 1919, following the deportation of the Egyptian nationalist leader Saad
   Zaghloul to Malta, Alexandria witnessed strikes and riots that resulted in the murder of
   several British nationals. British reprisals were severe, leading Forster to write a letter
   of protest to the *Manchester Guardian* on 29 March 1919 (*Life II*, 57).
18 Forster visited Thomas Hardy at Max Gate in March 1919.
19 Between 1919 and 1921, Forster reviewed books regularly for the *Daily Herald*, the *Daily
   News* and the *Nation & the Athenaeum*.

Victorians'[20] has fallen on to me out of the Times Book Club—I suppose he told them to send it.

Have you had a holiday yet? If not why not, Please write.

Yours ever
EM Forster

7

Harnham   Monument Green   Weybridge
25.4.19

Dear Cavafy

I am sending you an article on the poetry of C. P. Cavafy which I hope he will find bearable. I remember you told me that he would not disapprove of a few personal touches being introduced, so I have introduced some—I trust in tolerable taste. It makes such a difference to a foreign audience if they can feel they are being told some thing about the fellow.

And now, alas, I have to apologise to you both. The printers have made a devastating transposition of two lines—absolutely ruining one poem and enfeebling another.[21] At the bottom of the first column. You will see, you will only too clearly see. I have written to the editor (who admires the poems greatly): and I begged him to insert some sort of erratum or apology next week. If he does, I will send it you. I am frightfully upset. It has spoilt all the my pleasure in the article, which was very great. In fact I haven't had the spirits to read it through, lest I come on anything else.

Every kind of good wish.
EM Forster

---

20 Forster is likely referring to Lytton Strachey's *Eminent Victorians: Cardinal Manning, Florence Nightingale, Dr Arnold, General Gordon*, which was published in 1918. Warthan remains unidentified.

21 The poems referred to here are "The Sea of a Morning" and "Alexandrian Kings."

8

Harnham   Monument Green   Weybridge

9 – 5 – 19

My dear George

I have caused you to sign a letter[22] to the <u>Athenaeum</u>—jointly with me: I hope that's all right. We merely said, with pained dignity, that the printers had mucked two of Cavafy's poems. The <u>Athenaeum</u> has published it and reprinted the poems in full, and correctly. I have sent Cavafy a copy of the number.

Do send me some more translations, first revising them with him. I think I might be able to place some for him. Also do send me some of your own news. I'm all right, and very busy.

Yours

EM Forster

9

Alexandria

23 May 1919

10 Rue Lepsius[23]

Dear Forster,[24]

---

22 See plate 10.

23 Rue Lepsius was located in a rather déclassé section of Alexandria (the street was nicknamed "Rue Clapsius" owing to the presence of prostitutes). Cavafy lived over a brothel and in close proximity to both the Greek Orthodox Patriarchal church of Saint Savvas and the Greek Hospital of Saint Sophronios. Based on this intersection of the sacred and the profane, Cavafy was quoted as saying: "Where could I live better? Below the brothel caters to the flesh. And there is the church that forgives sin. And there is the hospital where we die" (Liddell, 180). See plate 5.

24 This is the second of two surviving drafts of this letter. The earlier draft, written on 22 May 1919, contains slight variations which show how meticulous Cavafy was about letter copying: "Dear Forster, Many thanks for the two copies of the Athenaeum, and for your kind letters of the 25th & 29th April. I liked the article <u>very much indeed</u>; and I feel so happy at your approbation of my poems. I hope you are in good health. I often think of you; and I am grateful for your friendship to me." Forster's letter dated 29 April (Cavafy's birthday) is lost.

Many thanks for your kind letters of the 25th & 29th April, and for the two copies of the Athenaeum. I liked the article <u>very</u> <u>much</u> <u>indeed</u>; and I feel so happy at your approbation of my poems. I hope you are in good health. I often think of you; and I am grateful, very grateful for your friendship to me.

Yours,
C. P. Cavafy

10

Weybridge   29–6–19

Dear George

Weeks and weeks and weeks ago the Athenaeum sent me your share of the article with the request that I would forward it to you since they did not know your address. This I never did. Comment is unnecessary. I only hope that Snelling[25] will not get to hear about it—it would furnish him with material for a very spicy pan. I enclose it the sum now (£ 2) with many apologies for my slackness.

Many thanks for your two letters and for the translation of Che Fece- - -.[26] I am sure that you think the remaining poems are not equally good. Do you think that you could work up Footsteps at all under Cavafy's eye? I enclose your version as it now stands. It is a good poem, I think, and I might see if the Athenaeum, which has been very pleasant about his work, will print it—though his poems, published without comment, certainly would be rather puzzling to an English audience.—Several of my friends have spoken to me with appreciation of our article, but I have not seen any references to it elsewhere in the press.

I hope you are keeping well. Are you never coming to England?

---

25 Snelling, presumably an editor, remains unidentified.
26 "Che Fece . . . Il Gran Rifiuto."

Lowes Dickinson[27] is stopping here. It is bitterly cold. Last night we had a fire.

Cavafy wrote me a nice note.

> Yours ever
> EM Forster

11

Harnham   Monument Green   Weybridge

13.8.19

Dear Cavafy

Furness[28] has given me a message from you which it was very kind of you to send. I have also to thank you for a letter. I am so glad that the article gave you any pleasure. I can never be sure how far the very clear image which—somehow or other—I have got of your work, corresponds with to the reality.

Alexandria often turns up in my thoughts and occasionally in the flesh. The other day Mrs Borchgrevink,[29] my mother, Furness, Dobrée[30] and myself had tea together after the Ballet. It was then, indeed, that your message came to me—shouted, to rise above the noise in which fashionable London now has its being.

---

27 Goldsworthy Lowes Dickinson (1862–1932), prolific author, fellow Kingsman, and close friend. Forster wrote Dickinson's biography in 1934.

28 Sir Robert Furness, a fellow Kingsman who introduced Forster to Cavafy, directed the wartime Press Censorship Department in Alexandria. He was an accomplished translator of ancient Greek poems, most notably those of Callimachus and *The Greek Anthology*.

29 Aida Borchgrevink was an American expatriate and bohemian socialite who once trained as an opera singer. She remained one of Forster's more memorable Alexandrian acquaintances.

30 Bonamy Dobrée was Professor of English Literature at Cairo University from 1926–1929 and a specialist in Restoration Drama. A mutual acquaintance of Forster and Cavafy, his name occurs frequently throughout their exchanges.

Do let me have a line if ever ~~your~~ you feel disposed. Also do tell George Valassopoulo to write: I am hoping he will send me some more translations.

Yours very sincerely
EM Forster

12

Harnham	Monument Green	Weybridge
	16/9/19	

Dear Cavafy,

Valassopoulo has sent me, to my pleasure, three more of your poems.[31] He says that you would like some of your work published in the Athenaeum, without commentary. This is exactly what I was hoping to effect, but the Editor is away for some weeks, and I must wait till he comes back. Meanwhile, it would be well if you could send me translations of some more of them, so that I can lay a greater choice before him. — I am not sure whether anything will come of this; but let's try, my dear Cavafy, let us try.

I was about to write in any case, as a great friend of mine, one Captain Altounyan,[32] is passing through Alexandria in October on his return to such a fatherland as the Armenians possess, and he wants to look you up. I have indicated your address, and 7.0. P.M.[33] as your most favourable hour. He is an engaging fellow—half Irish, and with literary tastes, though a doctor by profession.

With best wishes, as always; and how I wish you ever wrote a letter!

Yours ever,
E.M. Forster

---

31 See letter 10. The poems are "The God Abandons Antony," "Che Fece . . . Il Gran Rifiuto" and "Footsteps." To date, Valassopoulo's translations of the last two poems have not been located.

32 Ernest Haik Riddall Altounyan (1889–1962) was a doctor of mixed Irish-Armenian ancestry.

33 Cavafy's evening rituals for receiving guests famously involved the dramatic use of candles for creating a dimly lit interior (Liddell, 181).

13

Alexandria

10 Rue Lepsius

1 October 1919

My dear Forster,

~~Many thanks for~~ I received your letter of the 13th August, and I hope you will ~~pardon~~ excuse my delay in replying.

I asked of Valassopoulo to send you further translations of my poems. I am so glad you care to have more of them. ~~Regarding~~ In connection with your remark as to how far my work and the image you have of it correspond, I must say that, in as much as I think I perceive the latter, they do correspond. Besides, Valassopoulo's translations are so faithful that they facilitate a great deal the forming of an accurate idea of the work.

Our friend George Antonius has had a sad bereavement; his brother Michel died recently in Switzerland.

I daresay Furness will be back next month. Dobree, whom you mention, I met once; he came to my house a day or two before leaving the country. I liked him very much indeed. —

Your sincere friend,

C. P. Cavafy

14

P. & O. S. N. COMPANY'S
S.S. "Morea"

15.3.21

Dear Cavafy,

Creta Jovis magni medio jacet insula ponto,[34] and I cannot well pass it without reminding you of the fact. 'Cavafy's bit of the Mediterranean'

---

34 In *The Aeneid*, Book III (104–106), Virgil says of Crete: "If Jove assists the passage of our fleet,/The third propitious dawn discovers Crete" (John Dryden). Forster is on his way to India to serve the Maharajah of Dewas as private secretary. He will remain in Dewas through January 1922.

I said to myself when I saw the white ridge of Ida to the north, and felt (thank goodness) a little less inclined to be sick. Until Crete protected us the roughness was awful, far worse than Biscay's Bay's. Now, under benigner auspices, we are running to Port Said, and that is as near as I can hope to get to the Rue Lepsius for the present: For I go on from Port Said to Bombay, and at Bombay, if there is no railway strike, take a train to Indore, and at Indore take a motor or a ghari[35] or an ekka[36] or a string of black men, and reach Dewas, where some strange and vague but congenial job awaits me. There are two kings at Dewas. Each has his own tennis court and palace and army and láundry (just like Sparta):[37] in fact all things are separate except education, which owing to its unimportance is pooled. I serve the Senior Monarch, of course. He is an old friend of mine and an older friend of friends of mine, and if I manage not to fall ill I should have an excellent time. If you will write to me I will tell you about it. The Postal arrangements of the Dual Monarchy are somewhat confused, so I will give you the dull but sounder address of c/o Mess[rs] T. Cook and Sons, Bombay.

I have meant to write to you for so long. I was not able to place any of your poems because it is very difficult to place translations in the English Press, even when they are as good as George Valassopoulo's. I hope that you continue to write. As for my book on Alexandria, I have lost all interest in it.[38] The MS remains at in Chérif Pasha Street[39] and for ever will remain as far as I can see.

The maps (excellent) and the plans (quite good) have been prepared. Mann says he has spent £60 over them and I can quite believe it, for they are good work. But what is the use of maps and plans in an eternal state of

---

35 Ghari: an Indian carriage.

36 Ekka: a one-horse vehicle.

37 Forster is playfully alluding to the dual monarchy of ancient Sparta.

38 For the complex history of the composition and publication of *Alexandria: A History and a Guide*, see Miriam Allott's "Editor's Introduction" to the Abinger Edition of the text (Allott, lvi–lvii).

39 The posh street on which Whitehead Morris's publishing offices were located and also, coincidentally, the street on which Cavafy was born and where his family resided during their years of affluence.

proof? What is the use of my MS? And what, above all, is the use of Chérif Pasha Street? I wish, next time you walk down it, you would ask, in those tones of yours, that question - - - -

With kindest remembrances and best wishes.

Yours very sincerely
EM Forster

15

Harnham   Monument Green   Weybridge

7-7-22

My dear Cavafy,

I am bringing out in England at the end of the year a little book[40] — another book—about Alexandria, and I want to include in it the article about you that appeared in the Athenaeum. The publishers are also anxious that it should be included. Do you and does George Valassopoulo agree? I much hope so.

I met a young Menasce[41] at Oxford who enquired after you, and seemed intelligent and pleasant. But I am rather vague as to who he is.

Am well. Hope you are. Yours Britishly and forever.

EM Forster

---

40 *Pharos and Pharillon*.

41 Jean de Menasce, who, after studying at Oxford and the Sorbonne, converted to Catholicism and became a Dominican friar (Haag, 138–52). The Menasce family ran an international banking firm.

1. The Bourse Stock Exchange, Alexandria, site of the Sultan Hussein Club.

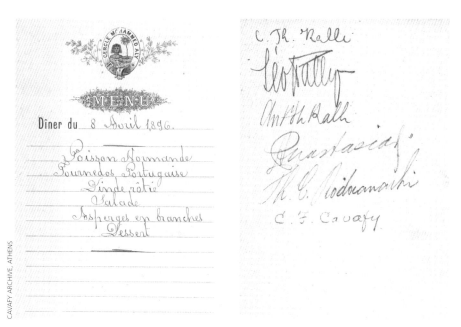

2. Menu from Club Mohammed Ali, where Cavafy first met Forster in 1916. Cavafy often dined here with his closest friends.

3. Cavafy at home, circa 1930.

4. Forster in Alexandria, circa 1917.

5. Cavafy's flat (third floor with balcony), Rue Lepsius, circa 1960.

6. Commemorative plaques outside Cavafy's home.

7. Cavafy's sitting room, where he received visitors.

8. George Valassopoulo in military uniform, circa 1912.

IRENE LIGHTBODY

9. Painting of the Valassopoulo "Villa Zancarol" in Rue des Fatimites, by Irene Lightbody.

10. Forster's letter to *The Athenaeum*.

11. Forster's home, "Harnham," Monument Green, Weybridge.

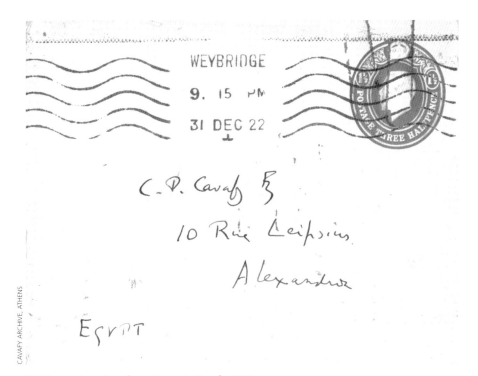

12. Stamped envelope from Forster to Cavafy, 1922.

16

Alexandria
10 Rue Lepsius
4 August 1922

My dear Forster,

Many thanks for your letter of the 7th July.

Valassopoulo and I are very glad of your intention to include in your fresh book the article about me: it will appear to more advantage there as that misplacing of verses (two lines of the poem "Alexandrian Kings") will have been set right.[42] The article I much like, as I wrote to you at the time, and as I told you when we met, early this year.[43] I have, however, one recommendation to make. Where you write of the poem "In the Month of Athyr"—the word "sixteen" to be replaced by "twenty-seven",[44] and, naturally, the word "boy" to be replaced by some other term.

The young Menasce, whom you met at Oxford, is a son of Baron Felix de Menasce. He is a very nice young man. He is now here on a two months' stay.

I am glad you are well; and I remain,

Ever Yyours
C. P. Cavafy

---

42 See letter 7.
43 Forster visited Cavafy in January 1922 while returning from India.
44 The confusion here has to do with Cavafy's use of the Greek letters "KZ" for 27 rather than Arabic numerals.

17

[My dear Forster,][45]

I pray excuse my being late in replying.

Many thanks for your letter of the . . .

Valassopoulo and I ~~will be~~ are very glad of your intention to include the article about me in your fresh book: where it will appear ~~needless It is needless to~~ to more advantage as that misplacing of verses ~~will~~ (two lines of the poem A. K.[46]) will have disappeared. The article I much like ~~a lot ; and though I all who came across it liked here liked~~ as I wrote to you at the time, and told you afterwards when we met, ~~last~~ early this year. I have however one recommendation to make. ~~Third colu~~ Where you write of the poem "In the Month of Athyr"— the ~~figure~~ word "sixteen" to be replaced by "twenty-six", and, naturally, the word "boy" to be replaced by some other term.

The young Menasce whom you met at Oxford, is, ~~I believe,~~ Jean de Menasce, ~~the son~~ a son of Baron Felix de Menasce. He is a very nice young man. He is here now ~~and took me.~~

I am glad you are well; I am in good health too. ~~xxx~~
~~Furness is in Alexandria; I do not think he will go abroad this year.~~
~~Dr Delta[47] who was feeling better has gone to Vienna, for a change of air and to consult a specialist on his health. He is feeling better. xxx~~
~~Valassopoulo xxx he is not here and will probably travel whether He will travel next year; he is very busy.~~
~~Mlle Miss Valassopoulo, his sister~~
~~Antonius came to Egypt in xxxx early~~

[C. P. Cavafy]

---

45 This is an unfinished draft of the previous letter which contains additional excised passages.
46 "Alexandrian Kings."
47 Dr. Constantine Delta (1872–1937) was the brother-in-law of the author Penelope Delta (1874–1941).

48   THE FORSTER–CAVAFY LETTERS

18

Harnham   Monument Green   Weybridge

31.12.22

My dear Cavafy

My Alexandrian Alexandria book[48] is out, but I am sending copies of it neither to you nor to George Valassopoulo nor to any of the friends who have helped me, the reason being that I shall send both to you and to George Valassopoulo and to the other friends ~~the~~ who have helped ~~help~~ me copies of my English Alexandria book which should come out next month, whereas I am sending copies of the Alexandrian Alexandria to friends who have helped me here.

The above sentence—nearly as long as one of your own though not alas similar otherwise[49]—should adumbrate to you the condition of my mind. But I am taking the greatest care in the correction of the proofs, and will remember my mistake about the young man's age in the Month of Athyr. The other mistake, the awful one made by the Athenaeum, cannot possibly recur in the book. I have put ~~the~~ 'The God Abandons Antony' between the two sections of the book (just as I put it between the two sections of the Alexandrian book). The arrangement is as follows: Title: PHAROS & PHARILLON

    Part I   PHAROS
                Pharos
                The Return from Siwa
                Epiphany
                Philo's Little Trip

---

48 *Alexandria: A History and a Guide*. The book's first edition reached a very limited circle of readers owing to the poor marketing strategy of the publishers and a subsequent fire at the publisher's storehouse in 1928. As it turned out, the books were spared, but because insurance money had been issued, they had to be artificially burned, a fiasco that led Forster to feel that the book had been jinxed. The "English Alexandria book" is *Pharos and Pharillon*.

49 Forster refers to Cavafy's notoriously long meandering sentences, which he playfully recreates in his first essay on Cavafy.

Clement of Alexandria
St Athanasius
Timothy the Cat & Timothy Whitebonnet

[The God Abandons Antony]

Part II   Pharillon
Eliza in Egypt
Cotton from the Outside
The Den
The Solitary Place
Between the Sun & the Moon
The Poetry of C. P. Cavafy

—I didn't mean to inflict all this on you when I started. Don't mention it (i.e. the details) to anyone, for the chief point of my tiny work goes ~~to~~ if it ceases to be a surprise.

With many many thanks for your help in both books.

Yours,
EM Forster

19

18-6-23   The Reform Club[50]   Pall Mall   S.W.

My dear George (as I always call you, I hope not impertinently)—

I received your letter with great pleasure. To whom should I send a copy of P. & P. if not to you? It is selling, you will be glad to hear, very well,

---

50 Forster joined the Reform Club—a gentlemen's club closely associated with the Liberal Party—in 1922. He was sponsored by Siegfried Sassoon (*Life II*, 134).

and indeed we expect to sell out the whole edition by next month. We have broken up the type, so shan't be reprinting I fear but we may import some sheets from America, where Knopf is issuing it. (All my publishers are Jews).

Give my love to Cavafy and tell him he owes me a letter. If he writes to me I shall send him some reviews which will interest and concern him. And if he does not write to me, I shall not send him the reviews.

Speaking seriously (and to you) his poems have caught the reviewers['] attention. You can't imagine how happy this makes me. I regard it as <u>most important</u> that you should translate some more. You've not only the literary ability but what's as rare—the mental honesty. A really important piece of work which none but you could perform lies under your hand, and I do urge you to set a little time aside, either from your legal or your social obligations, and to perform it. I would try to get the poems published in Magazines (I am in with some of the editors) and if I succeeded we might then think of a book. <u>I feel you owe this not only to Cavafy and yourself, but to Literature. If you don't do it, the (English speaking) world will be definitely poorer.</u> I have long meant to write to you on this point, and the reviews have stimulated me.

I suggest you translate the poem about the poet who is finding epithets for the ancestors of Mithridates (?) and then learns that war has been declared with Rome. I forget the poem's title[51]—am away from home. Start on this poem, and let me have it on or before July 10th when I shall be in town and can take it round to the editors.

All good wishes from

EM Forster

---

51 "Darius."

20

Harnham   Monument Green   Weybridge

5-7-23

My dear Cavafy,

   You are a bad poet. I have written to you and sent you two copies of the book[52] and a message vià Valassopoulo. Do I get a word in
reply? Not one word. You really must answer this. For things are rather
exciting. The book has had a great success for a book of its type. 900
copies have been sold in 6 weeks, we are rushing out a second edition; a
review of over a column in the Times Literary Supplement, long reviews
in the Nation, the New Statesman, the Daily Telegraph and so on. And
the things that have attracted most attention in it are your poems. The
reviewers have in some cases quoted them in full, and I have had private
letters—e.g. from Siegfried Sassoon[53]—anxious for more of them and for
more about you. And now I come to the exciting point. I was at Chatto
& Windus'[54] the other day—they are one of our leading publishers—
and they began asking me about you, and whether more of your poems
couldn't be translated. I didn't mention you, they did. Of course they
made no promise to publish and I don't want to raise hopes that may be
dashed. But seriously, my dear Cavafy, if you could get G.V. to translate
at once half a dozen more poems, I could then take them to Chatto &
Windus and talk over the matter again. If they were still encouraging,
we would add some more, and the end might be a nicely got-up book.
It's not much of an end, I know, still it would give you and G.V. and me
pleasure, and it would certainly give great pleasure to the discriminating
who read it. I hate it when beautiful things are kept from places where
they are needed. It makes me angry.

---

52   *Pharos and Pharillon.*
53   Siegfried Sassoon (1886–1967), a poet known for his war poetry, met Forster in March
       1922. His poetry is commented on favorably by Cavafy in letters 50, 54, and 71.
54   Chatto & Windus would eventually take the Hogarth Press under management in 1946.

Do you want to see some of the reviews? If you will be a good poet instead of a bad one I will lend you them. The Times[55] (by Middleton Murry I fancy, but it's unsigned) is really rather beautiful—semi mystic, semi humourous, and I think has 'got' us rather well. It sold us anyhow, like hot cakes.

Your expectant friend

EM Forster

21

10 July '23

My dear Forster,

I thank you warmly for "Pharos & Pharillon" which I appreciated very much indeed. Your essay on "Pharos" opens the book delightfully. I like the sentence, in the Return from Siwa, "The Greek Spirit". . . the Greek spirit still lived. But it lived consciously, not unconsciously as in the past." A vivid idea of second century A.D. Alexandria and of Christian Alexandria is given in "St. Clement", "St. Athanasius"[56] & the Timothys. Mrs Eliza Fay,[57] who introduceds the modern town, is most amazing. Very life-like "Cotton from the Outside", and your description of the Solitary Place is excellent. I need not repeat how much I like, and how grateful I am for, the article about my poetry.

Ever yours,

C. P. Cavafy

---

55 Murry writes in his review on 31 May 1923, "There is a vortex at Alexandria, and Mr Forster, being sensitive to these disturbances was drawn to it inevitably. That is how we would explain this book and the shimmering magic that dances in and out of its pages . . ." (Allott, 373–74).

56 On Cavafy's evident lack of sincerity here, and for the text of his own unfinished poem on St. Athanasius, see Introduction, p. 13.

57 Eliza Fay (1756–1816) wrote twenty-three letters documenting her travels in India. Forster's essay "Eliza in Egypt" opens the second section of the book, titled "Pharillon."

22

Harnham   Monument Green   Weybridge

1–8–23

My dear Cavafy,

Many thanks for your letter of July 10th. I must write to Valassopoulo too. After going through his translation of Darius with Furness, I submitted it to the Nation,[58] and it has been accepted with enthusiasm and by return of post! They offer £ 3-5-0, to which I have said that you agree— I hope I am right in so saying— and have told them to send you the cheque direct. I don't know when the poem will appear.

Here, you see, is a little source of income! Do cultivate it. Do select another poem (preferably a historical one) and get V. to translate it at once. It is important to keep your name before the public, now that interest has been aroused.

Yours ever

EM Forster

23

Harnham   Monument Green   Weybridge

4–8–23

My dear Valassopoulo,

Thank you so much for Darius. I made some trifling alterations (in your second version), and then sent it (together with the Greek original) to Furness for revision. Then I submitted it to 'The Nation'. It was accepted enthusiastically, by return of post, and will I hope appear in a few weeks. This entirely justifies my confidence in you and him, and now

---

58   Leonard Woolf was the literary editor of *The Nation & the Athenaeum* at the time.

of course I want some more. Is <u>The Displeasure of the Seleucid</u> good? I wish you would at once consult Cavafy, and translate either it or some other historical poem, and send it me as soon as you can. I remember too a poem about a sculptor,[59] which was subtle and interesting, but it may not translate effectively.

You ask for news of me. I am well, indeed inclined to grow fat, and my literary reputation also flourishes. God knows why, for I scarcely produce anything. <u>Pharos & Pharillon</u> (that little book I sent you) caught on surprisingly. It is now starting its career in America. As for my movements, I am just off to the wilds of the Scotch Highlands, but don't let that deter you from writing to me, for letters will be forwarded.

When are you coming to England? I think it is about time. It would be such a pleasure to see you again.

Yours very sincerely

EM Forster

I have told <u>The Nation</u> to send Cavafy the cheque (£ 3-5-0). I don't of course know what business arrangement, if any, you and he have made over the translating, so I leave you both to settle that question between you. —By the way I had quite a difficulty in convincing the 'Nation' that the poem was not your original composition! I didn't tell this to the poet in case it hurt his feelings! Your name will appear as the translator.

24

9 August '23

[My dear Forster,]

Many thanks for your letter of the 5<u>th</u> July, which I showed to G.V.

I am very glad ~~that~~ to hear your book has had such success and a ~~very~~

---

59 Most likely the "Sculptor of Tyana" although, to date, no trace of this translation has been found.

quite thoroughly merited success; and I am also very glad that ~~the~~ my poems have attracted some ~~notice~~ attention.

I wrote to you ~~in June~~ early in July and I ~~addressed sent~~ forwarded my letter to an address given to me by G.V.—The Reform Club.

~~Geor George~~ Valassopoulo has sent ~~to~~ you a translation of my poem "Darius"; also early in ~~June~~ July, I believe.

Have you seen ~~Forster~~ Furness at all ~~this year~~. He ~~was in~~ left for England ~~this year~~ this year; but ~~probably made xxx in London~~. I do not know whether ~~if~~ he intends to make a stay in London. I did not meet him ~~before he left~~ the days previous to his departure.

~~Besides it matter~~

Ever yours

[C. P. Cavafy]

25

Reform Club

London, S.W.

20.8.23

My dear Cavafy,

You fill my post bag this morning! First and best, a letter from yourself, then a proof of 'Darius' from the Nation, and thirdly a letter from the Hogarth Press[60] from which I quote:—

> "May we see the poems of Cavafy with a view to publication?
> It happens that we have nothing much on hand for the moment
> and we thought these so interesting that if the idea is practicable,
> we, on our side, would welcome it."

---

60 During 1923, the Hogarth Press expanded its output to produce eleven books, including Forster's *Pharos and Pharillon* and T.S. Eliot's *The Waste Land*. Between 1920 and 1940, Forster would publish seven pamphlets or books with the Hogarth Press.

It's obvious to me that if you can get your poems translated I can get them published in book form—either the by the Hogarth Press or by Chatto and Windus. I doubt your making any money over it—poems never pay in this muse-forsaken country—but you would be read by those who are capable of appreciating you. Furness can tell you all about the Hogarth Press. It is run by friends of mine. Chatto & Windus is a larger firm.

Can't you send me another poem by return for publication in a newspaper? This won't preclude subsequent appearance in a book.

Advance Alexandria!

Well my dear Cavafy, that is all for today. I write from the wilds of Scotland.[61] It pours. Do do send me poems. Am sending a line to Valassopoulo.

Yours ever

EM Forster

26

Postcard addressed to:

George Valassopoulo Esq

Rue des Fatimites

Alexandria, Egypt

20–8–23

Have just written to C.P.C. re an offer from the Hogarth Press to publish a volume of his poems. Perhaps you could very kindly talk it out with him. Excuse pc.[62]

EMF

---

61 Forster spent three weeks in Scotland during August 1923.

62 For a facsimile of this post card, see plate 18.

27

[My dear Forster,]

Many, many thanks for your two letters of the 1st & the 20th August. I am delighted that the translation of my poem "Darius" will appear in the Nation.[63]

In yr. letter of the 1st you asked for another translation; you must now have received it: V. sent you towards the end of last month a translation of the "Demaratus" a poem of mine which ~~was printed~~ appeared two years ago. I hope it ~~was~~ is to your liking.

I was a few days ago with V. (to whom of course I showed both your letters) and I believe he will take up another poem shortly. Unfortunately for the immediate furtherance by him of a larger number of translations, he is now, and has been last month, hard pressed with work; however, I understand that he looks forward to having again months not quite so full.

Furness is back, but I have not met him yet; I intend to go and visit him ~~one of these days~~ this, or next, week.

I hope your stay in Scotland ~~was~~ is pleasant, and that it didn't pour all the time as ~~it did~~ on the day you wrote me last.

[C. P. Cavafy]

28

Reform Club,
Pall Mall. S.W.1
17-9-23

My dear Cavafy,

I have been stopping with my friends the Woolfs this week end, and they tell me that they are writing you a business letter.[64] I hope that your reply to it may be a favourable one. If it is, would you care to entrust to me all

---

63 "Darius" appeared in *The Nation & the Athenaeum* on 6 October, 1923.

64 See letter 29.

the arrangements connected with the publication of the book? I should feel both pleased and honoured if you would, and I would try to ensure a volume worthy of you. —I don't of course mean that the matter would pass out of your control (you would see the completed translations fst before they were printed, also revise the proofs); but I think it would save time and trouble if there was someone in England who knew you and could assume a certain amount of responsibility in the matter, and I feel myself to be that person!

Meanwhile I anxiously await your reply to the offer to the Hogarth Press.

Yours ever

EM Forster

P. <u>Darius</u> has been held up in the <u>Nation</u> for lack of space but should appear next week. I will send you a copy.

Valassopoulo has very kindly sent me <u>Demaratus.</u>

29

THE HOGARTH PRESS

HOGARTH HOUSE   PARADISE ROAD   RICHMOND   SURREY

TELEPHONE: RICHMOND 496

C. P. Cavafy Esq
Alexandria

17 September, 1923

Dear Mr Cavafy,

The few translations of your poems which we have seen have interested us very much indeed, and we are taking the liberty of writing to you to ask whether you would consider allowing us to publish a small book of

59

your poems translated into English.[65] We are, of course, small publishers and the list of our publications is short; our experience of publishing books of poetry is that the sales are by no means large and not in proportion to their merits, but our books find their way to a small public who would, I think, appreciate your poetry.

I should explain that the books that we publish are sometimes printed by ourselves and sometimes we get them printed for us by ordinary commercial printers. We of course leave the matter entirely to you, but we should prefer, if possible, to print your poems ourselves, as in that es case we do not charge the cost of printing against the book at all. But if we printed it ourselves, it would have to be rather a small selection, not more than say 25 poems. The great advantage would be that there would be no financial difficulties in producing the book, while if it were printed for us, the costs of printing are still so high that it is difficult to produce any book of poems here without financial loss.

As to terms, we should offer you 25% of the profits and a small advance of £5 if we printed the book ourselves, and 2 33% of the profits if we got the book printed for us.

I hope very much that you will consider this favourably. If you do, will you be good enough to make a selection of the poems which you would like to be included. I understand that the best translator of your poems is in Egypt. Here of course again we would leave the matter entirely in your hands, but there might be some difficulty and delay if the translation were done in Egypt. On the other hand I think that, if you wished, we could arrange to get the translation done competently here and submitted for your approval.

Yours very truly

Leonard Woolf

---

65   This is the first publication offer made by the Hogarth Press to Cavafy. See letter 46 for the second.

30

Reform Club
S.W.

11-11-23

Dear Cavafy,

> All mourn, all deplore,
>   Both Gentile and Jew,[66]
> That they hear no more
>   From you.

> Yours inconsolably
> Fellow-Poet.

31

Harnham,
Monument Green,
Weybridge.

20-2-24

My dear Cavafy—

Young Menasce[67] has asked me to lend him such of the Valassopoulo translations as I possess, and I have done this, I hope rightly. I have also (I hope) placed another of the poems, 'The City' in the Nation.

---

66 Forster's playful reference to himself and Leonard Woolf betrays his growing impatience over Cavafy's delay in replying to the publishing offer.

67 Jean de Menasce (see letter 15, note 41), used his Oxford literary connections to place four of Cavafy's poems in the February 1924 issue of *The Oxford Outlook* ("Ionicon," "The Ides of March," "Manuel Comnenus," and "Come Back." Other notable writers included in this issue were Graham Greene (Sub-Editor), Cecil Day-Lewis (future poet laureate of Great Britain), and Robert Graves. The editor was C.H.O. Scaife, with whom Cavafy would collaborate on future translations between 1930 and 1932. "The City" appeared in *The Nation & the Athenaeum* on 5 April 1924.

If you will write me a letter authorising me to get some of your poems translated into English and published in book form, I will gladly do it, and save you all trouble, and I could probably arrange for it as well as Menasce could, since I am 'in' more with the publishers. But of course I can't (and wouldn't) move in the matter untill you give me the authorisation. Valassopoulo would have been the ideal translator but he will never do it now, he has delayed too long, and one must look elsewhere.

So do write me this—time!! I can't get a word out of you.

Yours very sincerely,

EM Forster

32

10 March 1924

My dear Forster,

Thank I thank you warmly for your letter of the 20th Febr, and I am apologise for my long silence (which made. You have done most rightly in placing Val's translation of the City with the Nation, and I am greatly gratified with the interest you, and the editor of the Nation, take show in for my work.

As regards Jean de Menasce, he told me, when he last was here in Jan. in Alex. and this year, that he would like to obtain fr. [fresh] Val. translations xxx one or two poems of mine, translated into English, for insertion in a periodical which appears at Oxford—he mentioned the name of the periodical,[68] but I do not recollect it now. Valassopoulo was very busy at the time, and could not supply the work; so it was arranged that on returning to England, Menasce would apply to you for one or two translated poems of mine for the purpose I just stated. Supplied Supplying to Jean de Menasce definitely Val. made (or remade) a translation of "Ithaca" I sent it to him last month.

---

68   *The Oxford Outlook* (see note 67 of previous letter).

I quite agree that Valassopoulo is the ideal translator. He has ~~just made into~~ finished ~~last week~~ an English translation of a poem of mine called "Caesarion" and ~~I understand that he has sent it to you~~ he sent it to you a ~~week ago~~ few days ago.

Last year he made and sent you a translation of my poem "Demaratus".

~~(The comple~~

~~I hope you are well..~~ I thank you, my dear Forster, for your friendship, which I ~~much~~ greatly value; and I remain

Ever Yours

[C. P. Cavafy]

33

11–3–24

HARNHAM,

MONUMENT GREEN,

WEYBRIDGE.

Dear Eliot,[69]

So pleased to hear from you again, and delighted to give the Criterion permission to publish anything of Cavafy it finds suitable. The poet's address is: C. P. Cavafy, 10 Rue Lepsius, Alexandria. The translator's: ~~G. Valassopoloulo~~ G. Valassopoulo, Rue des Fatimites, Alexandria. They have more or less left their English arrangements in my hands—while giving certain poems to de Menasce for the Oxford Outlook. It was a happy notion of his, writing to you. It hadn't occurred to me you would care for the stuff. I have just placed two with the 'Nation'—namely 'The City' and 'Theodotus'.

Can I be of any use? I can lend you the original Greek of any poem you select. Valassopoulo is honest, but clumsy and not always impeccable, and your ideal course, if you could persuade him, would be to get Arnold Toynbee to go through the poems. He has been so good as to do this for the 'Nation' couple, (I don't know him personally.)—(Failing this, I would

---

69 T.S. Eliot (1888–1965) was editor of *The Criterion*. Forster's tone here is curiously condescending toward both Cavafy (not thinking that Eliot would possibly "care for the stuff") and Valassopoulo ("honest, but clumsy and not always impeccable").

gladly try trimming them myself: for which I have no qualifications, but C. & V. do not mind.)

I heard from V. the other day, enclosing this revised translation of a poem which I think de Menasce has may have shown you. Please let make use of it if you wish—returning me the text at your leisure. As V. says, what on earth is to be done about the last words[70] (from Plutarch's 'Antony')? He can't translate it. I can't. Can you? The whole poem depends on it.

As for self, nothing is in my mind at all except how Coleridge[71] fell off his charger three times in a week, so was set instead to hold down a delirious comrade in a workhouse near Henley; and I don't feel there is the making of an article here, though it pleases me you should think of asking me for one.

With best wishes & thanks for your letter:

Yours sincerely
EM Forster

34

28-3-24

HARNHAM,
MONUMENT GREEN,
WEYBRIDGE.

My dear Valassopoulo,

Thank you so much for your letter and for the (revised) translation of Caesarion—you sent me a less finished rendering some time back: this is a great improvement, but, as you say, how shall we translate the final word?[72] It is excellent news that you are doing some more. I beg you and Cavafy

---

70 The last two words of "Caesarion" ("το 'Πολυκαισαρίη'") were rendered "Beware of many Caesars" by Valassopoulo.

71 This episode from Coleridge's life is recounted by Forster in the opening paragraph of his essay *Anonymity: an Inquiry*, which was published in 1925 by the Hogarth Press.

72 See the previous letter, note 70.

to work hard at it, because, as he gets better known, there is an increasing danger that some unauthorised person may push in, and turn out unsatisfactory renderings. That is why I am so anxious he should close with the Hogarth Press' offer, and should empower me to arrange as best I can: I should get you to translate as much as you had time for, and—if your work didn't allow you to do as many as I wanted—get someone else this end to translate the residue. But I can get no answer from Cavafy on this point: indeed, his continued silence makes me think that he is against the publication of any translations in book form.

Interest in his work continues to grow. I am lending one of the Greek originals he so kindly gave me to Arnold Toynbee—who was recently Professor of Modern Greek in London University. When he returns it, I must send it to T. E. Lawrence (the Arabian fellow)—who, by the way, greatly admires your translation. Then, the Nation has taken two more poems—'The City' and 'Theodotus', and T. S. Eliot has taken 'Ithaca' and possibly some more for the Criterion. Menasce sent them to him, but he very politely wrote and asked my permission to publish, which I gladly gave, for I was sure that you and Cavafy would be willing to appear in the Criterion: it is our best literary quarterly. —Then, as you probably know, Menasce has himself published four poems[73] in the Oxford Outlook but rather marred their effect by misprinting the poet's name![74]

You kindly ask about my own news. I am well, and—thank God!— have at last got my novel done. It appears in June. 'A Passage to India' is the title. I am now at a small piece of editing[75]—quite amusing. When it is done, perhaps I will go abroad. I meant to go this spring, but ten days' holiday in the West of England[76] seems to have set me up sufficiently. Besides, I don't know where to go. I hate Europe, and Africa and Asia are too far.

---

73 See letter 31, note 67.
74 Cavafy's name appeared as "Caravy." Menasce took the liberty of introducing an archaicizing idiom to the poems "Ionicon" and "The Ides of March."
75 Forster is editing Eliza Fay's *Original Letters from India (1779–1815),* which he published with the Hogarth Press in May 1925.
76 Forster traveled throughout Wales in early March 1924.

Best wishes. Please give the same to Cavafy. To receive a letter from either of you is always a pleasure to me: and better still if the letter is accompanied by a poem.

Yours very sincerely
EM Forster.

I have (with A. Toynbee's assistance) made one or two small alterations in your rendering of the two poems for the 'Nation' — I hope that's all right.

35

HARNHAM,
MONUMENT GREEN,
WEYBRIDGE.

14-4-24

My dear Cavafy,

Your welcome letter of March 14th [11th] took some time to reach me: it was delayed my end, not yours, apparently, being hidden under some papers by mistake, with the result that I have only recently opened it- should have written to you before, otherwise.

I hope that <u>The Nation</u> sent you the copy containing <u>The City</u>: also that you did not too strongly disapprove the slight modifications I made in the translation, with Arnold Toynbee's[77] authority. — But I have written on these & other points recently and at some length to Valassopoulo, so won't recapitulate.

I quite agree with you that Valassopoulo is your ideal translator if he would but ~~translation~~ translate! The British public won't know you as I wish, if he only sends a poem a year. Do urge him. The <u>Demaratus</u> was (from

---

77   On Toynbee's problematic role in Forster's translation project, see Introduction, pp. 17–18.

the English point of view) not quite as successful as the others, because the subtlety of the character didn't quite come through. But nearly all the rest he sent are excellent. I think I told him how much Colonel T. E. Lawrence admires your work and his: and L. is a good judge of literary matters.

More poems, then.

More poems.

I have at last finished my novel.[78] It will come out next month.

Tomorrow I am going to the Wembly [sic] Empire Exhibition to write an article for the Nation.[79] I believe it is all pools of water and open ~~dra~~ drains. I hope I shan't fall in, like—well, let us say like Sappho.[80]

His Majesty the King follows me there next week.

With all good wishes from your friend and admirer

EM Forster

36
Harnham—Monument Green—Weybridge

17-5-24

My dear Valassopoulo,

Many thanks for your two letters and the three poems.[81] I should have written before, but owing to the illness and death of an aunt[82] have been greatly occupied. Now I have much to say.

---

78 *A Passage to India.*

79 "The Birth of an Empire" was published in *The Nation & the Athenaeum* in 1924.

80 Sappho allegedly drowned after throwing herself off a cliff in Leucas in despair over the unrequited love for the boatman Phaon.

81 "Aimilianos Monai, Alexandrian, A.D. 628–655," "From the School of the Famous Philosopher," and "A Byzantine Grandee, in Exile, Composing Verses." These poems never appeared in *The Nation & the Athenaeum.*

82 Laura Forster died in May 1924.

I think the three poems superb. I have submitted them to the Nation which wants to publish them all, but asks me to do a little 'polishing'[.] I know that neither you nor Cavafy have any objection to my doing this, and have indeed instructed me to do it. But I am always rather nervous in case I carry the process too far. I will do my best. Possibly I may not let the Nation have all the poems after all, because it can only publish them with long intervals between. It may be better to arrange for them with the Criterion — which is a high-class literary quarterly. I will exercise my discretion.

The Nation has just sent me the proof of 'Theodotus' and please tell Cavafy that I will post him a copy of the number that contains it. Here, not only have I polished in my polishing, I have consulted Arnold Toynbee, formerly Professor of Modern Greek at London University, so we are jointly to blame for any misinterpretation.

You and Cavafy wonder how I can be paid for my labours. I can tell you! For each poem I succeed in placing, will you please send me translations of two more. This letter announces to you that I have placed four poems. So will you, my dear Valassopoulo, kindly send me by return of post translations of eight, and when I have placed these — and rapidly shall — I shall require translations of sixteen. This will keep you nicely busy.

As for de Menasce, the situation is a little difficult, because I sent him (with two or three exceptions) all the translations then in my possession, since I gathered from him that this was Cavafy's wish. He has duly returned the translations and has always behaved with complete civility towards me, but he has made typescript copies of the translations, and I don't know whether he intends to make any further use of these, either in the Oxford Outlook or elsewhere. If Cavafy is disinclined for him to do this, he had better write to him direct I think: I can't very well make any suggestion to him myself.

You ask about the erotic poems. But you've never sent me any! at least nothing that I recognised as erotic. I quite agree with you that they ought to be published, and I don't think that the British Public is as silly as it used to be on this point. It stands Aldous Huxley and D. H. Lawrence, and I don't imagine Cavafy will be hotter stuff than they are. Please let me know their names, because I rather fancy that, in the past, a letter to you of yours to me may have been lost, and that the poems to which you refer may have been included in it. Some of the poems you've sent me, I have not pressed on editors, it is true, but only because I felt the Greek did not probably quite come through in a translation[.] I have never held up ~~any~~ a poem because I thought it voluptuous or sordid.

Is not MIA NYXTA[83] (the poem on page 5) erotic? I have an idea that someone told me so. If it is, would you please send me a translation of it.

Arnold Toynbee has my duplicate copy of the poems, and he has promised to give me a list of those which are, in his opinion, particularly suitable for an English audience.[84] I will forward this on to you, in case it is any help.

Is there no hope you may come to England on your travels? I wish you would. You could meet the Hogarth Press people, and a discussion with them might prove very useful. If you don't come to England, what are your Continental plans? I have a faint hope of getting abroad also. A German friend[85] (a Pastor!) has asked me to stop with him in August in Berlin, and conceivably I might come south afterwards, and meet you. I am very busy at present with family matters, ~~and~~ so can't be certain of my movements, and my work has been knocked on ~~my he~~ the head entirely. It's lucky my novel is done. My publisher is giving me a dinner on May 28th.[86] All the leading booksellers of London are to be invited, and I am to make a speech, and the booksellers are to be so delighted with my speech that they are to order more copies of my book than they will be able to dispose of. At least that is the publisher's idea. Whether it will work, we shall see. Immediately after the dinner the book is to come out. In fact, it will correspond to the part played in a Roman Banquet by the emetic!

Please write to me, and at length, and so much the better if you send in your letter the eight new poems. I enclose an article[87] which has just

---

83 "One Night."
84 See letter 39.
85 Herr Steinweg who tutored with Forster at Nassenheide in 1905.
86 Edward Arnold hosted a book launch dinner for *A Passage to India*.
87 Hamish Miles published a review article on *Howard's End*, *Pharos and Pharillon* and *The Celestial Omnibus* in *The Dial* (Chicago: May 1924).

reached me from an American paper, and in which Cavafy is mentioned. I don't want it back. I will try to send you some more reviews of Pharos & Pharillon, but have none to hand. They have brought it out in quite a nice form in the States.

You will be about sick of this letter. I want in return for it all the Alexandrian gossip and news.

Yours ever
EM Forster

37

18 May 1924

[My dear Forster,]

I was ~~very glad~~ delighted to receive a letter (of the 14th April) from you.

~~I received~~ A copy of the ~~much~~ of the "Nation", ~~containing "The City"~~ in which "the City" appeared, reached me some weeks ago.

From ~~Jean~~ de Menasce I have not heard, ~~as I wrote to you on the ..., it was understood that I wrote to you about his demand to publish & C.~~ neither have I received a copy of the periodical in which he published the translations. ~~Do you happen to know which are the poems he published.~~

Valassopoulo has sent you translations of ~~the~~ my poems "Αιμιλιανός Μονάη, Αλεξανδρεύς . . ." and "Απ' την Σχολή του Περιωνύμου Φιλοσόφου."[88] I enclose the Greek originals.

I was very ~~glad~~ interested to read that you have terminated a fresh ~~volume~~ novel. ~~and I suppose that~~ I ~~can well understand how much work~~ suppose the getting it through the press entails much work: though, living out of, and far from, ~~a large~~ great literary centres my notions thereon are ~~apt to be~~ rather vague.

---

88 "Aimilianos Monai, Alexandrian, 628–655 A.D." and "From the School of the Famous Philosopher."

X It is most satisfying to me to know that Colonel Lawrence ~~has expressed approval~~ likes my poems. ~~Valassopoulo's translations of my poems and the poems~~

~~I am~~ I have read with much attention your ~~words~~ remarks on the poem ~~"Demaratus."~~

Ever Yours
[C. P. Cavafy]

38

10 Rue Lepsius
Alexandria
11 June 1924

My dear Forster,

I wrote to you last on the 18th May.

Valassopoulo has received your letter of the 17th May, & will write to you soon—he has been unusually busy of late.

I read with great satisfaction the article in the Dial[89] about you.

From Jean de Menasce I have still not received a word.—I am glad he has returned to you the translations, so that you, whose literary judgment I greatly value, may select what you deem is more appropriate for publication.

Valassopoulo has made two more translations of poems of mine. Πρέσβεις απ' την Αλεξάνδρεια (Envoys from Alexandria), and Υπέρ της Αχαϊκής Συμπολιτείας Πολεμήσαντες (Those who fought for the Achaean League). I enclose them with the Greek originals.

I am very, very thankful for the interest you take in my poetry; and the pains you take for making it known.

Ever yours,
C. P. Cavafy

---

89   See letter 36, note 87.

39

3, MELINA PLACE,
ST. JOHN'S WOOD,
N.W. 8.

Paddington 1508

12. June 1924.

Dear Forster,

I am afraid I have kept Kavafy [sic] a long time, but I have been reading him with great interest.

The poems fall into two distinct groups—erotic & historical, and
I suppose he would say that these two motives, between them, make
Alexandria.

He does seem to have got Alexandria into his bones, and I think it has
inspired true poetry in him—not bastard stuff, like most of the historical
poems that one knows.

He is an adept at the dramatic monologue, without Browning's over-
emphasis and elaboration. I admire the way in which he makes his point
by a series of flat colourless statements.

As to beauty of sound, I have come across nothing quite so fine (at
least, to a foreigner) as η Πόλις [The City].

Here is a list of a few which struck me as the best—but such choices
are very subjective:

1908–1914
Μάρτιαι Ειδοί [Ides of March]
Ιθάκη [Ithaca]
Αλεξανδρινοί Βασιλείς [Alexandrian Kings]
Φιλέλλην [Phil-Hellene]
Πολυέλαιος [The Chandelier]

1915
Οροφέρνης [Orophernis]
Η Δυσαρέσκεια του Σελευκίδου [The Displeasure of the Seleucid]

1917
Εν Πόλει της Οσροηνής [In a City of Osrhoene]
Εν Εσπέρα [In the Evening]

1918
Εις το Επίνειον [In the Harbour Town]

1919
Του Πλοίου [Of the Ship]

1920
Είγε ετελεύτα [Did he Die]
Ο Δαρείος [Darius]

So many thanks for letting me see them.

Yours sincerely
Arnold J. Toynbee[90]

---

90 Arnold J. Toynbee (1889–1975), British historian famous for his multi-volume study of
    the rise and fall of world civilizations *A Study of History* (1934–1961). See Introduction,
    pp. 17–18.

40

(as from: Harnham-Monument Green-Weybridge)[91]

My dear Cavafy,

Thank you for your letter of June 11th. I must apologise for my silence of late, but the illness and death of my aunt—followed by much business, and coincident with the appearance of my book—has left me very little time for my friends. Valassopoulo, to whom I wrote the other day, will perhaps have told you this, and he will also have given you certain messages from me.

Thank you also for the two poems you enclose (the 'Envoys - - - ' and '- - - the Achaean League').[92] They interested me much, though I do not think they are as suitable for an English audience as the two superb examples of your irony I last received (namely 'Emilianus - - -' and 'The Byzantine grandee - - -':[93] I hope to place these with <u>The Nation</u> when it has published the 'Theodotus'). The problem of suitability is rather a difficult one, and in this connection the list made by Professor Toynbee may be useful: I sent it to Valassopoulo. —The Demaratus—which I understand, and can well believe, to be among the sub[t]lest of your works—did not really get through in ~~your~~ the translation, I felt. —

I am stopping with T. E. Lawrence for a few days, and have brought down all your poems with me, that he may read them through. He has done so (all) with enormous enthusiasm. He said "A very great achieve-ment—~~work~~ modern literature of the very highest order in its class." Since he is well read in French and English—besides being a most remarkable personality and a fine scholar—his praise is worth having, I think: any how it gave immense pleasure to me. He also spoke highly of Valassopoulo's translations—though he added "But why doesn't Cavafy, with his perfect

---

91   Written from T.E. Lawrence's home at Cloud's Hill, Dorset, where Forster spent four days.
92   "Envoys from Alexandria" and "Those Who Fought for the Achaean League."
93   "Aimilianos Monai, Alexandrian, 628–655 A.D." and "A Byzantine Grandee, in Exile,
     Composing Verses."

knowledge of English, do his own translating?" He liked your 'flatness' as he called it: your 'chronicle-method' as I ~~called~~ call it: and he compares your final retrospective effects with the methods of Hérédia.[94] He said "I like the African & Asiatic poems best": I agree, as you know, but I should like to have some examples of your ~~mo~~ erotic poetry also, so that all aspects may be represented. — By the way, when sending in the future, do not trouble to enclose the originals, because, when last we met, you very kindly gave me two complete sets. One I keep at home, the other I lend about.

You were kind enough to enquire about my book.[95] I am glad to be able to tell you that it has made an excellent start. Both the press and private criticism has been favourable, and the sales go well. My publisher gave a dinner, at which various booksellers and myself were present; somewhat of an innovation, ~~which~~ but it has worked quite well from the advertising point of view. He has also brought out a special edition of 200 signed copies, in the hope that we shall find 200 rich men who are sufficiently foolish to buy them. I fear not: wealth finds other outlets for its imbecility. It is more to the point that Thomas Hardy was over here yesterday and ~~cheered~~ delighted me by a word of praise.[96]

I must conclude this scrawl. Thank you very much for your thanks! It makes me very happy to think that I may have been able to introduce you to a few new readers. I am sure that your work will have a European reputation in the end, but it will take time. All good things take time.

Believe me with admiration and affection,

Yours ever

EM Forster

T.E.L. is in thorough sympathy with your <u>language</u>.

---

94 José María de Hérédia (1842–1905), French Parnassian poet.
95 *A Passage to India*.
96 Thomas Hardy (1840–1928) praised *A Passage to India* which he had been reading aloud to his wife Florence (J.H. Stape, *An E.M. Forster Chronology* [London: Macmillan, 1993], 87).

41

Alexandria

10 Rue Lepsius

1 August 1924

My dear Forster,

I received your letter of the 25th [23rd] June.

I can well understand how little time to spare you must have had—with the sadness of a bereavement, and all the cares it entails, and this just at the time of the appearance of your book.

Valassopoulo is not here. He has left for Greece. I expect he will be back in three weeks, as his partner, A. Skenderani, is leaving for Italy towards the end of August.

Certainly "the problem of suitability" is a difficult one; and I feel completely secure in your experience for the choosing of what would be more likely to interest somewhat the British public—or, to abate, the section of it that might care to know my poetry.

<u>Of course</u> Colonel Lawrence's approbation is worth having—most worth having.

I am indeed <u>very glad</u> for the great success your book has obtained. I liked the innovation of the dinner.[97] I congratulate you on Thomas Hardy's praise of your novel.

I was vastly pleased to see "Theodotus" in the "Nation"; and I thank you for the copy of the number you sent me; also thanks for the intimation that "Ithaca" appeared in the "Criterion".[98] Furness called last week, and he told me how excellent a review the "Criterion" is. It is very satisfactory to me that a translation of a poem of mine figures in the pages of this periodical.

Ever yours,

C. P. Cavafy

---

97 See letter 36.

98 Also featured in the July 1924 number of *The Criterion* were W.B. Yeats, Virginia Woolf, and Hugh Walpole. See plate 14.

42

2-1-25

My dear Valassopoulo,

Your letter fills me with great excitement. We <u>must</u> meet. Is it impossible you should come to London? Do try to. How long must you remain in Paris? Let me know at once. I want to talk over the whole Cavafy business, and I want you to meet some publishers and discuss things with them on his behalf. Heinemanns[99] are after him now—I heard yesterday.

I want too to see you for my own sake. It would be a great pleasure. Do manage it.

I do hope your brother is benefiting from the treatment—I don't suppose he will remember me, for I only saw him once (and thought him so nice): please give him my kind regards if he does remember me.

Every sort of good wish to yourself, and looking forward to our meeting keenly. Get on with those translations like hell! Now's your time.

Yours very sincerely
EM Forster

Oh yes—am quite famous, so please see me at once while it lasts.

---

99 Heinemann publishers.

43

2-1-25

My dear Cavafy,

A happy New Year to you, both Greek and non-Greek. But chiefly to say that I have (I hope not wrongly) given your address to Mess[rs] Heinemann the publishers at their request. I expect that (if you do ever publish in England) you will go to the Hogarth Press, who are pleasanter people: still there seemed no harm in putting you into touch with Mess[rs] Heinemann—I told them I knew nothing of your present intentions, so you are quite free.

I am much excited by a line from Valassopoulo in Paris: he says he is getting on with the translation, and I am urging him to do so, and shall if it can possibly be arranged see him and talk.

I have been meaning to write before, but have been rather occupied and worried by domestic affairs. My book (you will rejoice to hear, like the good friend you are) does well, and has had a great sale in America, and is coming out in Sweden, Czecho Slovakia and France. All good wishes from

EM Forster

44

8-1-25

My dear Valassopoulo

I am so grieved to hear of your mother's illness:[100] I thought in your

---

100 Irene Valassopoulo, *née* Zancarol (1871–1925).

previous letter that you spoke of your 'brother', but perhaps I misread the word. Do come to England if you possibly can, I have rooms in town and I can put you up if you do not mind living very simply. Even if I am not with you all the time, you can have the rooms—indeed you will be more comfortable if I am not with you, for there will be more room.

If it proves absolutely impossible for you to come to England, I will try to come to Paris for a day or two, but it is not easy for me to get away, as we are shifting houses.[101]

We <u>must</u> meet—not only for our own pleasure, but in the interests of Cavafy. It is, as you say, most important that we should have a good talk about the poems. Yes, please do send me the rough drafts of the poems. As to the erotic poems, I agree entirely with Cavafy: they must be translated without any softening if they are done at all. Please send me one or two specimens of them—I asked you to do so before, but you didn't—! Then I can tell whether the English public will stand them. I expect it will be all right. <u>Literal</u> translations mind.

My own book is being translated very beautifully into French,[102] but I have not found a publisher in that country for it yet. Do you know of one? I have arranged in Czecho-Slovakia and Sweden—curious that those countries should come first. I am negotiating in France, Germany and Denmark. Sales in the U.S.A. now touch 35,000. Please excuse this swash. It is not swash really—I only know how kind you are in taking interest in my success, and remember how once I read part of a draft of the book to you and Antonius many years ago.[103]

Best of wishes: and WE MUST MEET.

Write again and send the rough drafts at once.

        Yours sincerely

           EM Forster

---

101 In 1925, Forster inherited the lease of his aunt Laura's house West Hackhurst in Abinger Hammer near Dorking. The house was designed by Forster's father. See plate 23.

102 *A Passage to India* was translated into French by Charles Mauron (1899–1963), the French critic with whom Forster established a close friendship.

103 See letter 2.

45

Alexandria

10 Rue Lepsius

16 January 1925

My dear Forster,

I was very glad to receive a letter (2nd January) from you. I wrote to you last on the 1st August. Many thanks for a the copy of the Criterion (July) which you sent me.

You are quite right in your remark about the Hogarth Press. I am very grateful for their kind communication to me in September 1923.

I am glad at the good tidings you give me of your book. —I have read—and reread—"A Passage to India". It is an admirable work. It is delightful reading. I like the style, I like the characters, I like the presentation of the environment, I like the attitude. I was <u>charmed</u> by this book. I keep it by me. Very often I take it up and read over again now this part of it, now that.

Valassopoulo ~~remains~~ is still in Paris; I telephoned to his office yesterday: they expect him to be back towards the end of this month.

I saw your portrait[104] in the Illustrated London News (11 October) and in the Graphic (8 November); and I am made happy by your success.

Ever yours,

[C. P. Cavafy]

46

THE HOGARTH PRESS[105]

52 Tavistock Square, London W.C.I.

Telephone: Museum 3488

C. P. Cavafy Esq

10 rue Lepsius

Alexandria

---

104 Forster's portrait was done by William Rothenstein in 1923.
105 This is the second offer made by the Hogarth Press. See letter 29.

1 September, 1925

Dear Mr Cavafy,

I have been speaking again with Mr E. M. Forster about an edition of your poems. I have also seen the translations by Mr Valassapoulo [sic] and read them with the greatest admiration. I am now writing to urge you very strongly to allow us to publish these translations in a volume which we will have printed for us. We would offer you a royalty of 10% on the published price or, if you preferred it, one-third of any profits made from the publication, and in any case we would pay an advance of £10 on the day of publication.

I hope that you will consider this proposal favourably.

Yours very truly
Leonard Woolf

47

Alexandria
18 September 1925
10 Rue Lepsius

Dear Mᵣ Woolf,

I received your letter of the 1ˢᵗ Sept., and I am <u>greatly pleased</u> that my poems, in Mᵣ Valassopoulo's translation, have met with your approval. I am also very grateful to Mᵣ Forster who has repeatedly shown so much interest in my work.

Mᵣ Valassopoulo (to whom I showed your kind letter) has indeed made translations of a good many of my poems, but he and I now find that they require a careful revision, and that revision we are engaged upon. As soon as 25 translations of poems are completed and copied, Mᵣ Valassopoulo intends sending them to Mᵣ Forster.

One point which I wish to emphasize is that I am fully alive to the importance, as regards my poems, of your favourable notice of them.

Yours very sincerely

C. P. Cavafy.

48

West Hackhurst   Abinger Hammer   Dorking
                        27/9/25

My dear Cavafy,

I do hope that I have done right, but Harold Monro,[106] the editor of the 'Chapbook' and himself a poet of some standing, ~~and~~ has urged me to let him have something of yours, and though in the ordinary course I should have refused such a request (for I think it better for your fame that your poems should appear, when appear they do, in book form) yet I thought it better to accede on this occasion, since the 'Chapbook' has a cachet about it, and will be read by people whose judgment you would respect. Hence the enclosed.[107] It is going to press now. I have carefully revised the English under the supervision of Colonel Lawrence, and I hope ~~I have~~ we have done nothing contrary to the wishes of Valassopoulo or yourself.

You will of course receive a copy of the magazine. The rates of payment are I fear very moderate, but I have told Monro he must send you £2, and I hope they will arrive, though poetlike (?) he has made no reply. I have given him your address. His address is The Poetry Bookshop, 37 Devonshire Street, W.C.

---

106 Harold Monro (1879–1932) was a British poet and the proprietor of The Poetry Bookshop in London.
107 Forster enclosed a copy of "One of their Gods."

I have just had the pleasure of a letter from Pericles,[108] to which I must reply. He sends me the interesting and welcome number of 'Nea Techne'.[109] I am so glad that you cared to have my little article reprinted in it.

Thank you for the letter you wrote me some time back, and please excuse my typewriting. It is not that I am becoming more efficient (perish the thought!), but that I broke my wrist in the spring, and typing is easier than writing—though I suffer no pain.

All good wishes from

EM Forster

49

10 October 1925

My dear Forster,

Your letter of the 27th Sept. gave me much pleasure. You did quite well in sending a translated poem of mine to the "Chap. Book", and I am ~~much~~ greatly beholden to you for this mark of friendship. I am also thankful to Mr Monro[110] who expressed the wish to ~~publish~~ insert in his magazine ~~"One of Their~~ a translation of "One of their Gods". ~~Publication~~ I much value publication of translated poems of mine in English periodicals. ~~I much val~~

X ~~Publications of t. poems of mine in English periodicals I much value.~~

---

108 Pericles Anastasiades (1870–1950), an aesthete and amateur painter, was a close friend of Cavafy who worked with Robin Furness in the Press Censorship Department during the war. Forster tutored him in English while serving in Alexandria.

109 *Nea Techne* ("New Art") was a leading Greek literary journal published in Athens. In 1924, an entire issue (July to October 1924) was dedicated to Cavafy—the first journal to pay him tribute. Publication of the journal, which included a Greek translation of Forster's essay on Cavafy, was delayed until early 1925.

110 Harold Monro was responsible for launching many major twentieth-century poets and authors. The 1925 issue of the *Chapbook* featured the work of Leonard Woolf, Conrad Aiken, H.D., Wyndham Lewis, Jean Cocteau, Robert Graves, and Aldous Huxley, among others.

I have had news of you from Valassopoulo early in the year, and from Pericles[111] lately; and the seclusion in which I live does not prevent of my hearing of your great success in letters.

The "Nea Techne"[112] have been very good to me; I was much gratified to see ~~by their~~ from their special number (of July—October 1924), as well as from articles in daily papers, that I have many ~~more fervent~~ warm friends in Athens.

I enclose three translations by V. of poems of mine ~~which Valassopoulo and I have revised carefully. These are~~ The Tomb of L[anes], O[rophernes], In the C[hurch]. These translations have been carefully revised by him & me. I also enclose the Greek originals.

I was sorry to ~~hear~~ read you hurt your wrist in the Spring: I hope ~~it is~~ you are under no serious inconvenience by now.

Pericles ~~tells me to send~~ sends his warmest regards, and was very glad to hear that you will write to him.

Ever yours,

[C. P. Cavafy]

50

Alexandria

10 Rue Lepsius

8 December 1925

Dear Mr Monro,

Many thanks for the Chapbook. It was very kind of you to send me a copy. I was ~~charmed~~ delighted by it. ~~I liked both the text and the illustrations.~~

I read your verses with the greatest interest, and I much appreciated them.

Exquisite the lines

---

111 Pericles Anastasiades (see previous letter, note 108).

112 See the previous letter, note 109.

"Your beauty makes me cringe in fear[,]
And flinch, as I have always done,
When some bright danger glittered near
Or eyes were dazzled by a sun."[113]

—

"I've found you standing just outside
My body's door."[114]

I like Mr Sassoon's[115] "To an Old Lady, Dead" ("Old Lady, when last time I sipped your tea. . . . ."; "Now you are a very strange old lady, stiff, sacrosanct, and alabaster-faced"). In "Alone"—"how strange we grow when we're alone, and how unlike the selves that meet[,] and talk." I am fond of Mr Sassoon's poetry. I recollect reading—some years ago—beautiful lines of his in the "London Mercury."

I like Mr Frank Strange's "Over my ways the trees may ponder, Waving their dark green fingers like fools".[116] Very forcible Mr Fletcher's "for in truth you were bearing the black sins of Europe."[117]

I like In Mr Alec Brown's "Citizens at a Citizen's Funeral". I like the introduction of exclaimings "ah, what shall be done, ah what shall I do"; "alas what can I know"; "alas what can I do."

The opening article by Mr Woolf[118] is very good indeed excellent. Most interesting are Mr Aldington's remarks on free Free Verse (for note, his quotation from Milton).[119]

---

113 Lines from Harold Monro's "The Romantic Fool."
114 Lines from Harold Monro's "Great Distance."
115 Siegfried Sassoon (see letter 20, note 53).
116 Lines from Frank Strange's "Here are the Needed Ways."
117 Lines from John Gould Fletcher's "To Columbus."
118 Leonard Woolf's essay is titled "Obscurity."
119 Richard Aldington cites the following lines from Milton's "Preface" to "Samson Agonistes": "The measure of verse used in the chorus is of all sorts, called by the Greeks Monostrophic, or rather Apolelymenon, without regard had to Strophe, Antistrophe or Epode—which were a kind of stanzas framed only for the music . . . or being divided into stanzas or pauses, they may be called Allaestropha."

The engravings, the drawings are charming. They commence most fittingly for me—who am so far away—with Mr Ginner's showing of the Bookshop.[120]

I enclose the Greek text of "One of their Gods"; It may be you would care to see it.

My kindest regards to Mr Forster, to whom I am under obligation for many marks of friendship.

Yours faithfully,

[C. P. Cavafy]

T.P.B. [The Poetry Bookshop]
35 Devonshire Street
Theobald Road
London W.C.

51

Station Gomshall

West Hackhurst,

Abinger Hammer,

Dorking.

10-12-25

Dear Cavafy

The enclosed is from one of ~~the~~ our leading younger poets:[121] he has just got the Professorship of English Literature, under the Egyptian Govt. I have given him the introduction he asks for, as I am certain you will like him—he is most charming, and original to the point of wildren.

The Chapbook is out, but I have not seen a copy yet.

Yours ever
EM Forster

---

120 Charles Ginner's drawing of Monro's The Poetry Bookshop.

121 Robert Graves (1895–1985), English poet, translator, and novelist, took a position at Cairo University in 1926. See letter 52.

52

Dear Forster,[122]

Your recommendation, for which many thanks, has helped to get me that Cairo job. Salary not as good as it pretended: but good—We were amazed to hear you were near here recently but without means of transport: Nancy[123] would have fetched you gladly. We sail Jan. 8$\underline{th}$: en masse. Any chance of seeing you before then? I read your <u>Anonymity</u>[124] with great pleasure: but not always agreeing. I want an introduction to Cavafy before I go.

Yours ever
Robert Graves

53

Alexandria
10 Rue Lepsius
10 December 1925

The Hogarth Press
52 Tavistock Square
London

Dear Sirs,

I received your letter of the 16$\underline{th}$ November,[125] and beg to thank you for it. I am sorry I am a little late in replying, but I have been unwell for a few days.

---

122 This transcription is made from Cavafy's handwritten copy of Graves' letter.
123 Nancy Nicholson (1899–1977), British painter, married Graves in 1918.
124 See letter 33, note 71.
125 The letter enclosed a contractual agreement for publishing Cavafy's poems.

I return, enclosed, both forms of the Memorandum of Agreement, which you kindly sent me. I have made, however, and kept a copy for future reference.

I am much beholden to Mr Woolf for the interest he showed for my work, in its translated form.

If I did not sign ~~one of the copies~~ of the Agreement, it was because I considered that my signing it would be premature.[126]

Mr Valassopoulo and I are revising the translations, as I wrote to Mr Woolf on the 18th September.

I forwarded to Mr E. M. Forster, with Mr Valassopoulo's consent, three ~~copies of~~ translations of poems of mine,[127] on the 10th October. Apart from these, Mr Forster has previously received seven revised translations: some were sent to him by Mr Valassopoulo; some by me, with Mr Valassopoulo's consent.

As soon as fifteen more are ready (or twenty five, if Mr Forster considers—which, however, is not likely—that all the ten above referred to should be superseded) they will be sent to Mr Forster—agreeably to what I wrote to Mr Woolf on the 18th September.

I might mention that the designation of the work, on the enclosed forms, had better have been "Poems, written in Greek, by C. P. Cavafy; translated by G. Valassopoulo".

I cannot terminate this letter without saying that I am very grateful to Mr Woolf and to Mr Forster for their great friendliness to me.

I should be glad if you would obligingly show this letter to Mr Woolf.

Yours faithfully,
C. P. Cavafy

---

126 For Cavafy's comments on the agreement, see Introduction, note 44.
127 See letter 49 for the titles of the three poems.

54

Alexandria

10 Rue Lepsius

11 December 1925

My dear Forster,

I received a copy of the Chapbook,[128] and I liked it very much. Your recommendation of it to me, in your letter of the 27th September, was fully justified.

I enclose five more translations (with the Greek originals) of poems of mine. ~~which~~ Valassopoulo and I have carefully revised them. They are "The Tomb of Lysias the Grammarian," "Young Men of Sidon, A.D. 400," "In a City of Osrhoene," "The End," "Demetrius Soter (B.C. 162-150)." I wrote to you last on the 10th October, and sent to you with my letter three revised translations.

~~I hope you are well. In your last letter (of the 27th September) you mentioned a painful wrist said that writing was still inconvenient owing to an accident to your wrist in the spring. But that inconvenience must now be, I trust, a thing of the past.~~

There is much character in Monro's poetry. These, in the Chapbook, are the first verses of his that I read.

I am very fond of Siegfried Sassoon's poetry. ~~I liked, particularly, his verses "To an Old Lady, Dead."~~

You probably know that Mr Woolf wrote to me about the issuing of a ~~volume of~~ volume of translations of poems of mine. I wrote to him saying that Valassopoulo and I are now revising the translations, and that they will be sent to you in their revised form. I was glad of this opportunity which gave me occasion to tell Mr Woolf how much I prized his favourable opinion of my work.

Ever yours,

C. P. Cavafy

---

128 See letter 50.

55

23 December 1925

My dear Forster,

I received your letter of the [10th December] . . . . , and I return the letter of Mr Graves to you. I was very glad gratified by Mr Graves' caring for an introduction to me, and delighted was very glad that you gave it. Mr Graves is not unknown to me. I read lines of his in the Chap. book, full of vigour; and I came across poems of his in the London Mercury of 1921. I wrote to you last on the 11th October December; previous to that, I wrote to you on the 10th October (enclosed with that letter I sent you translations of three poems of mine "Orophernes", "In the Church", "The Tomb of Lanes";[129] carefully revised by V. & me). I return Mr Graves' letter to you.

Ever yours

[C. P. Cavafy]

56

STATION GOMSHALL

WEST HACKHURST,
ABINGER HAMMER,
DORKING.

2-1-26

My dear Cavafy,

Many thanks for your letter of Dec. 23. Those of Dec 11th and Oct. 10th were also safely received, and I am carefully keeping the poems they enclosed until you come to some decision as regards publication. I am glad that you know Graves' work. He is a lively lad and should make officialdom sit up. He is looking forward to calling on you.

All best wishes for the New Year[.]

Yours ever

EM Forster

129 See plate 13.

57

STATION GOMSHALL   WEST HACKHURST,
                                          ABINGER HAMMER,
                                          DORKING.

20-1-26

Dear Cavafy,

This introduces my friend Mr Crawford Flitch[130] — traveller in Spain and elsewhere—writer—friend of Unamuno—talk to him. He will give you news of me, and my best wishes.

Yours ever
EM Forster

Alexandria
10 Rue Lepsius
9 March 1926

My dear Forster[,]

I received your letter of the 2nd January, in its time; and on the 1st March I received a few lines of yours (dated the 10th [20th] January) introducing Mr Crawford Flitch. I was really glad to ~~know~~ make the acquaintance of Mr Flitch. He is most interesting company. Unfortunately he stayed but very little in Alexandria. He intended leaving, as he told me, on the 3rd for Constantinople. It is most considerate of you to give me the opportunity of knowing friends of yours. I look forward to a call from Mr Graves, who is now in Cairo.

I enclose two poems of mine translated by Valassopoulo, and revised by both him and me. They are "The Tomb of Ignatius" and "Monotony"

---

130 J.E. Crawford Flitch was a friend and translator of the Spanish poet, novelist, and philosopher Miguel de Unamuno (1864–1936). His translation of Unamuno's *Tragic Sense of Life* appeared in 1921.

(they are accompanied by the Greek originals).

I have been ill all through January, and part February, with an inflammation of the left eye. I am now, however, well.

Ever yours,
C. P. Cavafy

59

STATION GOMSHALL

WEST HACKHURST,
ABINGER HAMMER,
DORKING.

28/3/26

My dear Cavafy,

Please excuse a line, and a typed line, in reply to your welcome note; since breaking my wrist, I have tended towards typing. Thank you, in the first place, for the poems; I shall shortly be writing at length to Valassopoulo about them—he also has sent me some more poems. Then—secondly—I am so glad that you liked Flitch.[131] I think he is a really interesting fellow, though this is not always observable at a first meeting; I don't know, by the way, why you say it is considerate of me to give my friends introductions to you; considerate to them it is indeed, for having read your work they are only too anxious to meet you! I have just heard from Raymond Mortimer;[132] much disappointed that the shortness of his stay in Alexandria did not enable him to call.

I am so very sorry to hear that your eye has been so troublesome.

All good wishes from
EM Forster

---

131 See letter 57, note 130.
132 Raymond Mortimer (1895–1980), British writer and critic.

60

My dear Forster,

I received, in its time, your letter of the 28th March.

I have been troubled afresh by my left eye; and a small operation had to be performed. I am now well.

A friend of mine pointed out to me a number (of the 6th March) of the "Les Nouvelles Littéraires" (Paris) which contains an article (by André Maurois[133]) on the English novel of today. I was glad to read it. The writer's comment on "A Passage "A Passage to India" (that excellent work) is judicious. "Quand Forster nous montre dans Passage to India des Mahométans, des Hindous, des Anglo-Indiens, ce n'est pas pour nous convaincre que les uns ont raison, que les autres ont tort, que les uns sont bons, que les autres sont mauvais, non, ils sont ainsi, voilà tout."

I daresay you have seen George Antonius[134] (I met him on the day he was leaving for England, and I begged of him to remember me to you). Furness has also left for England early in May this month. I dined with him at the Club Mohammed Ali on the 29th April.

I enclose two further poems of mine—"Of the Jews (50 A.D.)", and "The Tomb of Eurion"—translated by Valassopoulo, and revised by both him & me. (I also enclose the Greek originals).

> Ever yours
> [C. P. Cavafy]

---

133 André Maurois, pen name of Émile Salomon Wilhelm Herzog (1885–1967), French author and prolific literary critic.

134 See letter 2, note 4.

STATION GOMSHALL

WEST HACKHURST,
ABINGER HAMMER,
DORKING.

19-1-27

My dear Cavafy,

I am giving an introduction, I hope not rashly, to a young man I scarcely know, but he is obviously intelligent and mutual friends say that he is nice. His name is Christopher Scaife[135] and he is coming out in connection with the Egyptian Gazette. He was at Oxford – President of the Union there, I believe, which is, among undergraduates, a notable honour. Since then he has been on the West End stage. I know not with what success. He is well educated and intellectual. He will probably present his introduction pretty soon, for he seemed very pleased to get it, and I hope that your health may allow you to receive him.

I am well and very busy with lectures, which start this week—I forget whether I told you that I am Clark Lecturer at Cambridge this year, a somewhat agitating honour, and have chosen "Aspects of the Novel"[136] as my subject. There will be 8 or 9 lectures. It is a Trinity lectureship, not the an University one, but something of a public function, because people haven't to pay to get in.

Dobrée,[137] whom you knew slightly, has just gone to the professorship of Cairo which Robert Graves vacated. I wonder whether you will see him. Graves had a touch of genius, but Dobrée is doubtless better suited to the post, and he is also quite a scholar, and a specialist on the subject of the Restoration Drama.

---

135 C.H.O. Scaife, lecturer in English Literature at the Royal University of Egypt in Cairo, was the editor of *The Oxford Outlook*. He received the Newdigate Prize in 1923 for his poem "London." His memorial poem to Cavafy titled "Epitaph" appears in his volume *Towards Corinth O Englishman* (London: Cobden-Sanderson, 1934): "Do not bring laurel here, or tears,/But, if you have some beauty turn/And greet your lover—/This is Cavafy's urn" (5). For his collaboration with Cavafy on translations, see Introduction, note 65.

136 *Aspects of the Novel* would be published in 1927 by Edward Arnold.

137 See letter 11, note 30.

I went abroad this summer, but to Denmark and Sweden: a great success.

I do hope that your eyes trouble you less. They were not well when last you wrote.

All best wishes,   Yours ever   EM Forster

62

My dear Forster,

I ~~was delighted to~~ received a ~~your letter from~~ of ~~you~~ the 19th January; and was glad to have news of ~~news~~.

The Clark Lectureship you call "a somewhat agitating honour". ~~But I find that~~ Still, — ~~though at such a distance, and with so little~~ limited a knowledge ~~of the Clark's literary life — that it is best it is an honour~~ it appears to me, that it gives you an excellent opportunity ~~for you~~ for to ~~expressing~~ your views on the "novel". Sometimes one ~~expresses with more freedom literary~~ finds a lecture a more convenient channel for expressing ~~literary views~~ opinions than an article in a review; even if one knows that the lecture will ultimately be printed.

~~Denmark & Sweden must be very interesting to see. Have you picked up anything of the language Danish.~~

Dobree I ~~certainty~~ met some years ago; but not since. Robert Graves ~~never came~~ did not come to see me, though he had a letter of introduction from you. But ~~perhaps~~ it may be he did not visit Alexandria ~~at~~ I regret this, as I ~~liked~~ read several poems of his which I much liked, and should have been ~~glad of his~~ happy to make his acquaintance.

Mr Christopher Scaife[138] I have not yet seen. ~~You did very~~ I am very glad you gave him an introduction to me. I ~~am delighted~~ like to make the

---

138 See letter 61, note 135.

95

acquaintances of people you know. ~~I mentioned Mr. Scaife's name to Jean~~
~~de Menasce, and he said he knows him.~~

Furness, as you ~~perhaps know~~ probably are aware, is in Cairo. He ~~came~~
~~to~~ spent in Alexandria ~~last month~~ for a few days last month, and he ~~called~~
came to see me an afternoon along with Pericles[139] and Aristide Pally.[140]
~~On~~ It happened that the [. . .]

Nicholas Cazantzaki[141] same afternoon ~~a very~~ a distinguished man of
letters from Athens (only on a ten days stay in Alexandria) came to my
house; and ~~N C spent~~ I was ~~happy to make~~ glad to make him known to
Furness, and Furness to him.

[C. P. Cavafy]

63

20 . 5 . 28

My dear Cavafy,

I am very ashamed of myself: a letter from Furness has made me realise my shortcomings. I vaguely thought I had told you that Eliot was
delighted to get your poems, and bade me say he would use them if the

139 See letter 48, note 108.
140 Unidentified but likely a member of the Pally family that resided in Alexandria.
141 Nikos Kazantzakis (1883–1957), the Greek author, visited Cavafy for a few hours in
   1927 and recorded the following impressions: "He should have been born in fifteenth-
   century Florence, a cardinal, the secret confidant of the Pope. . . . Now as I see
   him for the first time this evening and hear him, I feel how wisely such a complex,
   heavy-ladened soul of sanctified decadence succeeded in finding its form in art—a
   perfect match—in order to be saved. . . . Cavafy has all the formal characteristics
   of an exceptional man of decadence—wise, ironic, hedonistic—a charmer with a
   vast memory. . . . Seated in a soft armchair, he looks out the window, waiting for the
   barbarians to arrive. He holds a parchment with delicate encomia written in calligraphy,
   dressed in his best, made up with care, and he waits. But the barbarians do not arrive,
   and by evening he sighs quietly, and smiles ironically at the naiveté of his own soul
   which still hopes" (Nikos Kazantzakis, *Journeying: Travels in Italy, Egypt, Sinai, Jerusalem
   and Cyprus*, trans. Themis and Theodora Vasils [Boston: Little, Brown and Company,
   1975], 56).

<u>Criterion</u> remained above ground. It is surviving, and no doubt your poems will appear in due course.[142]

At any rate I hope I told you how much I liked them myself. They are admirable—as are all the poems of yours that I have read.

Please forgive my delinquencies.

Yours sincerely

Bonamy Dobrée[143]

64

13 June 1929

My dear Forster

I thank you <u>warmly</u> for what you wrote about me in the "Semaine Egyptienne."[144] It is a fresh proof of your friendship which I greatly prize.—Though I live at so great a a very considerable distance from England, tidings reach me of your great, and merited, success literary success; and I am gladdened thereby. I heard, this year, an excellent lecture by Bonamy Dobree on your work.—Perhaps you will meet see Dobree soon in London. He sailed for Greece last week: his stay there, however, was to be quite a very short one.—I daresay you saw Furness: his four Greek

142 The poems "For Ammones, Who Died at the Age of 29 in the Year 610" and "If He Did Die" appeared in the *Criterion* of September 1928.

143 See letter 11, note 30.

144 *La semaine égyptienne* was a Cairo literary review. Forster contributed an article "Dans la rue Lepsius" (translated by Charles Mauron) to a special edition dedicated to Cavafy in April 1929.

lines were delightful.[145] —Two of my poems appeared (translated) in the Criterion[146] last year. ~~It was much~~ They gave me intense satisfaction ~~at that~~. I wish ~~to~~ you would ~~repeat this~~ say so, from me, back to Mr Eliot when you meet him.

Ever yours,

[C. P. Cavafy]

65

8-7-29

Union-Castle Line

S.S. "Llandovery Castle"

My dear Cavafy,

A great pleasure to receive your kind letter. Shall I find you in Egypt about Sept. 10th or 14th? It is just possible I might stop there a day or two on my return from South Africa, and I am much more likely to stop if there is the chance of seeing you. Please will you send a line ~~to~~ as soon as possible to:

E.M.F.
> British Association
> Passenger SS Matiana
> c/o Mackenzie Smith & Co.
> Mombasa, British East Africa.

---

145 Robin Furness contributed the following epigram to *La semaine égyptienne* in honor of Cavafy: "Ελλάδος εν στεφάνω περιπύστων άξι' αοιδών/των τόθ' εής σοφίης άνθεα λεπτολόγου/ηδυεπής επέπλεξεν, Αλεξανδρείον άγαλμα,/ημέτερος ΚΑΒΑΦΗΣ, — "βαιά μεν, αλλά ρόδα." [Our sweet-voiced Cavafy, the glory of Alexandria, who wove together the flowers of his delicate wisdom, equal in worth to the famous wreathed poets of ancient Greece—"the flowers are few—but they are roses."] Furness is imitating Meleager and the epigrammatic tradition of *The Greek Anthology*, which he knew well as an accomplished translator.

146 See previous letter, note 142.

I am just starting this rather ambitious tour.[147] This letter will be posted to you on the remote island of Ascension.

Always your friend
EM Forster

66

[8.8.29]

My dear Forster,

Your letter of the 8th July (which I received yesterday) has made me happy.

I have no intention of leaving Alexandria this year; so I shall have the great satisfaction of seeing you again. I am looking forward to it. Immediately you arrive in Alexandria, let me know, please.

I am very glad at the news.

Ever yours,
C. P. Cavafy

67

LUNA PARK HOTEL   TELEPHONE NO. 15-92 MEDINA
KAMEL STREET   TELEGRAMS: "LUNAHOTEL"
OPPOSITE COOK'S OFFICES
CAIRO, EGYPT

Cairo, 14-9-1929

My dear Cavafy,

All goes well, and if it continues to go so, please expect me on your door step Tuesday at 9.0. I got your letter at Mombasa. Thank you so much for it.

Yours ever
EM Forster.

---

147 Forster was invited by Florence and George Barger to travel to South Africa on a cruise organized by the British Association.

68

P & O.S.N. Co.
S.S. Narkunda
26.9.29

My dear Cavafy,

I have just sent off the copy of the S.E.[148] to the Jennings Bramlys,[149] an— I was not able to dispatch it earlier—and I have already lost a second copy to old Dr Green,[150] a crusty but not unaimiable [sic] Egyptologist. I lent it him, he became extremely interested, and he wanted to show it to Wace[151] and other archaeologists in the British Museum who know modern Greek. So I thought I would let him keep it for that purpose.

(Private, this)

I wish I could have stopped longer.[152] There was so much to say, and I quite forgot to tell you that I have written a novel and some short stories which cannot be published, and which I should like you to have seen.[153] But you would have to come to England to see them, and this you will never do!

I was delighted with my stay in Egypt, and with the kindness of all my friends, and am firmly resolved to come again. I hope the Tachydromos article[154] went well; as a rule I refuse to be interviewed, but of course I

---

148 *La semaine égyptienne.* See letter 64, note 144.
149 Major Wilfred Jennings Bramly, former District Commissioner of the Western Desert, built a desert settlement for Bedouins at Burg el Arab near Abousir. His daughter Vivian later assisted Forster in revising the text of *Alexandria: A History and a Guide* for its second printing in 1938 (Allott, lxii).
150 Frederick William Green (1869–1949), Egyptologist.
151 Alan John Bayard Wace (1879–1957), archaeologist.
152 Forster visited Cavafy for a few hours in September 1929.
153 Forster is referring to *Maurice* (1971) and the homoerotic short stories posthumously published in *The Life to Come* (1972).
154 Forster was interviewed by Rika Singopoulo for the Greek Alexandrian newspaper *Tachydromos* ("The Postman"). For the full translated text of the interview, see Hilda Spear, ed., *Forster in Egypt: A Graeco-Alexandrian Encounter* (London: Cecil Woolf, 1987).

wanted to fall in with anything connected with Singopoulo[155] — he was so nice to me when I was out before — not to mention anything connected with you. Valassopoulo has promised to send me a copy of the article.

I shall write again from England. It is very easy for me to communicate with T. S. Eliot and as for the two new translations[156] you of have given me, I shall try to place one of them in the <u>Nation</u>. Your new long poem pleased me much,[157] and as translated by you, had to my mind the quality of a poetic short story. (I say 'as translated' because, could I read it in the original, it would, I know, have purely the quality of a poetic poem!).

Here I am on another piece of paper, with nothing to say except that I admire your work more than ever, that I loved seeing you, and that it is very cold. We reach Marseilles tomorrow. I attempt to meet an Indian friend[158] who is returning to India. No doubt he will make a muddle of it.

And the dinner bugle has blown, and though I do not intend to change my clothes I must at all events wash my face, so goodbye for the present.

With much affection and thanks from

EM Forster

69

Alexandria
10 Rue Lepsius
15 October 1929

My dear Forster,

Your letter of the 26<u>th</u> September from on board gave me great pleasure.

---

155 Alexander (Alekos) Singopoulo (1898–1966) was Cavafy's confidant, heir, and literary executor. He and his wife Rika lived in the flat beneath Cavafy during the poet's last years. Rika was the editor of the literary journal *Alexandrini Techni* ("Alexandrian Art"); she and her husband brought out the first Greek volume of Cavafy's poetry in 1935, two years after the poet's death. See letters 77–79.

156 These translations were given to Forster in person and no written trace of them exists.

157 "Myres: Alexandria 340 A.D."

158 Unidentified.

Your stay here was too short, and I am glad to read you contemplate coming to Alexandria again. The hours we were able to spend together were too few: our friendship required more. At least, during these few hours I had the opportunity to express to you fully my admiration for that beautiful book "A Passage to India", to explain the reasons for my admiration. They have become, ever since 1924, companions of mine:—Mrs Moore, Fielding, Aziz, Adela, Heaslop, the Nawab Bahadur, McBryde. I walk into the Club, and am get much agitated by the "women and children" ϱήματα.[159] I am in Heaslop's house and listen, knowingly, to "red nine on black ten,"[160] which of course pertains to the patience, but is also indicative of a firm decision to keep out of the inane mess.—

The interview appeared in the "Tachydromos"[161] of the 26th September, and Mme Singopoulo tells me she has sent you two copies of the issue. She also tells me that the portrait of yours by Rothenstein[162]— "Graphic" 8 November 1924—was chosen because she had been informed by the "Tachydromos" that they could not obtain a satisfactory print from the other—"Illustrated London News" 11 October 1924.

I am <u>delighted</u> at your intention to place in the "Nation" one of the translations of my poems;[163] and I am glad it is easy for you to communicate with Eliot.

If you see Dobrée, remember me to him, please.

Ever yours,

C. P. Cavafy

---

159 Modern Greek for "clichés."
160 See *A Passage to India*, chap. 22, where Mrs. Moore plays patience while blurting out her opinion on Dr. Aziz's innocence.
161 See letter 68, note 154.
162 William Rothenstein drew Forster's portrait in 1923.
163 No future poems would appear in *The Nation*.

STATION GOMSHALL

WEST HACKHURST,

ABINGER HAMMER,

DORKING.

24–8–30

My dear Cavafy,

I was at Arles the other day with my French translator and friend, Charles Mauron,[164] and he told me of an inscription in the Aliscamps which, he said, always reminded him of your work—he admires you greatly. So we went out to see it, and it reminded me also, and I am sending you a small monograph in which it is quoted—though I don't think it is transcribed quite correctly, and the translation is most certainly incorrect.

I have owed you a letter for ages, ages, and ages, but you have known me for ages that are even longer, and may therefore be sure that you never pass from my mind. I have not much news about myself. I am well, and at present busy preparing some more lectures for Cambridge on the subject

---

164 Charles Mauron (1899–1966), the French critic who translated *A Passage to India* into French. Forster dedicated his *Aspects of the Novel* to him. The inscription mentioned here is from *Les Villes D'Art célèbres: Nîmes, Arles, Orange, Saint-Rémy* (Paris: Librairie Renouard, 1929): "Aeliae Aelia[nae]/litteram qui nosti, lege casum et d[ole puellae?]./ multi sarcophagum dicunt quod cons[umit artus],/set conclusa decens apibus domus ist[a vocanda]./o nefas indignum, iacet hic praecla[ra puella],/hoc plus quam dolor est, rapta est specios[a puella],revixit virgo, ubi iam matura placebat,/nuptias indixit, gaudebant vota parentes./vixit enim ann(os) XVII et menses VII diesque XVIII./o felicem patrem qui non vidit talem dolorem,/h(a)eret et in fixo pectore volnus Dionysiadi matri,/et iunctam secum Geron pater tenet ipse puellam." [You who are literate, read the maid's misfortune and feel pity. Many refer to it as a sarcophagus because it devours the body but what should we name this beautifully wrought tomb that encloses honey bees? Ineffable misfortune: here lies this radiant girl, a fact which is beyond sadness. The snatching of a beautiful girl, who lived her life a virgin. Nearing the age of marriage, she announced her nuptials. Her parents rejoiced. She lived 17 years, 7 months and 18 days. Blessed is the father who never sees such sadness. The pain remains in the wounded soul of Dionysias the mother, and her (dead) father Geron continually keeps the girl near him.]

of 'The Creator as Critic.'[165] They interest me pleasantly, and entail much agreeable reading, but I wish I was inventing something. Novels and stories no longer form in my mind, and I suppose that, at my age, if that process once ceases it will never recommence.

Woolf[166] has left the <u>Nation</u>, so that I have not had the opportunity of suggesting your two poems there. I wrote to Eliot, and reminded him that he had something of yours, but I don't know whether he has done anything. He is a curious creature, and attacked me for no conceivable reason in the press the other day.[167] But I rather like him.

After my behaviour, I can't expect any early reply to this letter, but later on if you would send me a line about your work and yourself I'd feel grateful. I did so much enjoy my last visit to Alexandria, and have vague ideas—I don't know whether they will mature – of coming again in about a year's time. Please give my affectionate remembrances to Valassopoulo when you see him, and please accept the same for yourself.

Yours ever
EM Forster

71

29.9.30

My dear Forster,

I was delighted to receive a letter from (of you: your letter of the 24th August.

---

165 Forster would deliver this series of lectures at Cambridge University between January and March 1931. They were recently published in Jeffrey Heath's *The Creator as Critic and Other Writings by E.M. Forster* (Toronto: Dundurn Press, 2008), 64–98.

166 Leonard Woolf.

167 This literary spat centered around Forster's claim in a letter to *The Nation & the Athenaeum* (29 March 1930) that D.H. Lawrence was "the greatest imaginative novelist of our generation." Eliot wrote a letter the following week countering with "I submit that this judgment is meaningless" (*Life II*, 163–64).

Many thanks for "Nimes, Arles, Orange, Saint-Remy" by Roger Peyre. The inscription[168] you ~~write of~~ mention is ~~most~~ very interesting.

I was glad to ~~hear~~ read that Mauron likes my poems.

Yes; though I do like receiving letters from you, I <u>know</u> <u>well</u> that the lack of them by no means denotes ~~that~~ any diminishing of your friendship for me.

~~Any letter is welcome; from you is welcome: but one more especially like this I have of the 24th August, which contains much the excellent reading intimation~~ I read with great pleasure in your letter that you have it in your mind to come if possible, ~~to come~~ next year to Alexandria.

I am sorry ~~to read~~ that your relations with Eliot are not as ~~friend~~ cordial as before. But I am in hope it is but a passing cloud.

I am not at all sure you are ~~write~~ right when ~~you say that because~~ after saying that "novels and stories no longer form in my mind" ~~and I suppose~~ you ~~rather surprisingly~~ deduce that the process will not recommence. Why? Is there not such a thing as temporary cessation?

I daresay your Cambridge lectures will require of you a ~~lot~~ good deal of work. Do you intend to publish them later, in some periodical, or in book form? ~~I wonder what your lectures if I understand aright from the title "The Creator as Critic." Is it I take it to mean the criticism which is applied by the artist to his own work or in some production? This critical faculty is an excellent thing: its drawback, I consider, but slight, and worth the risk: it is that the being overcritical of his productions works leads him to produce less; but then if he is a sound critic he won't be overcritical.~~

I have printed this year three poems. They were reproduced by a review of Athens, the "Protoporia."[169]

Valassopoulo wishes to be remembered to you.

~~Did~~ Have you seen Furness at all?

~~Do you occasionally see Siegfried Sassoon? I like his poetry.~~

---

168 See letter 70, note 164.

169 The three poems printed in 1929/1930 are "He Asked About the Quality," "The Mirror in the Front Hall," and "To Have Taken the Trouble."

~~Bonamy Dobree is~~

If you chance to meet Bonamy Dobree, please remember me to him.

> Ever yours,
> [C. P. Cavafy]

72

14-5-31

My dear Cavafy,

The enclosed may perhaps interest you, so I forward it, as the writer[170] suggests. He is a young South African, who has, for the love of it, learnt some modern Greek: an unusual youth, I think, and finding he hadn't read you[,] I lent him my duplicate of your early poems. I think I shall have to let him keep it—his admiration is certainly genuine—and I must certainly lend him the duplicate of the later poems, also.

Plomer's novel, <u>Turbot Wolf</u>[171] [sic], and his short stories <u>I Speak of Africa</u>, interested me a good deal. He left his native land in disgust for Japan, and has also written about Japan,[172] but I haven't read him on that subject, nor do I know his poems, except one about Ulysses returning to Corfu,[173] which I liked. He is a large fair creature, with a reserved precise manner which contrasts oddly with the little I know about his life. I think if you cared to write to him, it would give him enormous pleasure.

I have been meaning to write to you myself: you are often in my thoughts, but this you know. I owe you a letter: and this <u>I</u> know. Such news as I have

---

170 William Plomer (1903–1973), South-African poet, novelist, and librettist for Benjamin Britten. In 1960, Forster asked him to write his authorized biography, but later relegated the project to P.N. Furbank.

171 *Turbott Wolfe* (1925).

172 Forster likely has in mind Plomer's volume of short stories *Paper Houses* (1929) and his autobiographical novel *Sado* (1931), which involves a relationship between an Englishman and a Japanese.

173 The poem "Corfu" appeared in Plomer's volume *The Fivefold Screen* (London: Hogarth Press, 1932), which also included the poem "Sonnet to Cavafy" (see Appendix, p. 188).

is good. I have just finished a tiny little piece of work[174]—only 6000 words, but it pleases me. I shall send you a copy of it when it's printed.

I write from Belfast of all places, so I haven't your letter to refer to. I get home again in about a week. I write at once, in order to effect the young man's introduction to you: I know he's impatient for it.

> With all good wishes as ever
> from
> EM Forster

73

95 Warwick Street S W 1
11 May 1931

Dear Forster,

Do you think it would be possible for me to obtain a copy of the Poiemata[175] of Cavafy? If not, I must take copies of several before I return you the book, for they give me a great deal of pleasure. So much so, in fact, that I have written a sonnet by way of tribute to their author. If you don't find it excessively commonplace, and if you think there is the slightest chance of its pleasing Cavafy, I wonder if you would consider forwarding it to him next time you write?

> Yours,
> William Plomer

If you're in London at all next week, will you perhaps have lunch with me? I shd like you to meet—if you wd care to—a friend of mine who is an admirer of yours, a Frenchman called René Janin.[176]

---

174 "A Letter to Madan Blanchard."
175 Greek for "poems," the title of Cavafy's poetic collections which he circulated privately.
176 René Janin was the son of a famous French general and member of Plomer's London circle of dilettantes.

74

My dear Forster,

Many thanks for your letter of the 14th May. I am glad to hear that you have added fresh work to your ~~excellent~~ admirable previous ~~work~~ production; and shall be delighted to read it.[177]

I was much interested in all you write about William Plomer,[178] and it was very good of him to write the verses ~~to me~~ about my poetry which you sent me. I ~~am writing~~ have written to him, & I enclose the letter. Will you oblige me by handing it or forwarding it to him, as well as the copies of my poems (Collection 1905-1915; & Collection 1916-1918) which I send (to your care) separately. ~~Please~~ I thought it safer to communicate through you. On Plomer's note to you, there is an address Warwick Street; but then, I am not sure whether it be not but a temporary one.

E. Y.

[C. P. Cavafy]

~~Furness went to Skyros on the occasion of for the inaugurals of the monument to Rupert[179]~~

75

Alexandria

10 Rue Lepsius

1 June 1931

Dear Mr Plomer[180]

---

177 Cavafy refers to Forster's "A Letter to Madan Blanchard."

178 See letters 72, 73 and 75.

179 A memorial was erected to the poet Rupert Brooke (1887–1915) on the Greek island of Skyros. Forster would later resign from P.E.N. over his objection to its commercial promotion of a travel brochure featuring a cruise to Skyros for the unveiling of Brooke's memorial (*Life II*, 173).

180 See letter 72, note 170.

It was very gratifying to me to ~~hear~~ understand from Mr Forster that my poetry has given you pleasure. I thank you warmly for your verses to me which I much liked. I am very proud of them. I am sending you— through Mr Forster—a copy of my Collection of Poems 1905–1915, and one of my Collection of Poems 1916–1918.

Yours faithfully,

C. P. Cavafy

76

12.1.32

My dear Forster[,]

I was delighted by the "Letter to Madan Blanchard".[181] Lee Boo[182] is a personality of rare refinement: ~~one likes to read of, that might appeal to one likes to try and picture to one's self.~~ "he embraced civilisation with the grace of a courtier and the integrity of a curate": "ultra-civilized to the last".

I hope you are well and I wish 1932 will be a year of happiness for you.

[C. P. Cavafy]

77

Station Gomshall   18–6–33   West Hackhurst,

Abinger Hammer,

Dorking.

My dear Singopoulo,[183]

I have been intending to write to you some time, and now Furness tells

---

181 See letters 72 and 74.

182 Forster's letter is based on an account of the Palau Islands composed from the journals of Captain Henry Wilson in 1783. In a colonialist attempt to annex the Palau Islands, the British bring Prince Lee Boo back to England to be educated. Cavafy's quotes are from this essay.

183 See letter 68, note 155 and my Introduction, notes 57 and 58.

me that you desire us both to arrange, if we can, for a complete English translation of Cavafy's poems.

I feel it a very great privelege [sic] to be trusted with such a task, and I shall do my best to fulfil it adequately. I am writing now, in particular, to tell you this.

I want also to express my sympathy with you and your wife in your great loss,[184] and my deep appreciation of all that you have done for our friend. I think that, ever since he met you, his life became happier, and what he would have done in his last years without the devotion of you both, I cannot imagine.

Furness, or I, will probably be writing again to you shortly, in connection with our projects.

Believe me with every kind remembrance to you both,

  Yours v. sincerely

   EM Forster

78

STATION GOMSHALL   7–11–36   WEST HACKHURST,

                  ABINGER HAMMER,

                   DORKING.

Dear M[r] Singopoulo,

You will think me strange in so long delaying to thank you for the magnificent gift of three copies of Cavafy:[185] but I have not long received them, since Furness, who brought them for me to England, has only recently handed them to me. I am most grateful to you, and it is particularly good of you to have included an edition de luxe. I propose to give one of the copies to a library—probably to the London Library, where it will be accessible to those who will appreciate it.

---

184 Forster is alluding to Cavafy's death on 29 April 1933, the day of his seventieth birthday.
185 Alekos and Rika Singopoulo brought out the first Greek edition of Cavafy's complete poems in November 1935. One of Forster's copies was inscribed in French by Rika: "Pour M. E. M. Forster avec toute mon estime."

I am glad to say that the possibilities of publishing an English translation are still very good. Mr John Mavrogordato[186] has already translated over 70 of the poems, and hopes to complete the work by the end of the year, and Messrs Chatto & Windus, the publishers, write that they retain their interest in the scheme. I hope therefore that you will now think the time suitable. I believe that Mr Furness may be writing to you about this, also.

With all kind remembrances to Madame Singopoulo and yourself, and thanking you very ~~wary~~ warmly: Yours sincerely

EM Forster

It was very good of you to inscribe one of the copies.

79

STATION GOMSHALL   21–1–37   WEST HACKHURST,
                                                       ABINGER HAMMER,
                                                       DORKING.

Dear Mr Singopoulo

I have now got detailed estimates from Messrs Chatto & Windus for printing 1000 copies of Cavafy's poems. I will not trouble you with a long letter until I have had a reply to this one, but will just summarise the result. For publishing 1000 copies of the English translation only, they ask (about) £100; for publishing the Greek with the translation opposite (about) £170. I consider these estimates as very moderate, and shall be glad to hear your opinion. Mr John Mavrogordato has now completed the translation, which strikes me as excellent.

---

186 John Mavrogordato (1882–1970), Professor of Modern Greek at Oxford University. For the delays related to his translation, see Introduction, note 58.

I am writing by the same post to Mr Furness: possibly he will be seeing you to discuss the matter.

Yours sincerely
EM Forster.

80

28 Rue Cherif Pasha
Alexandria February 2$^{\underline{nd}}$ 44

My dear Forster,

I apologise for having neglected you for so long, I hope that you are well and I am sure that you have become very famous by now.

As you will see from the enclosed passages I am working hard at something definite on Cavafy, I am translating <u>all</u> the historical poems and a fairly good few of the others and hope to have finished in about 5 or 6 months. This time it's going to be a serious business.

I have obtained Mr Singopoulo's[187] approval but there is, apparently, a hitch, as he appears to have entered into some sort of agreement with Mr Mavrocordato, on your side, for the translations.

Would it be possible to propitiate Mr M. by allowing him as well as yourself, for services rendered, a reasonable percentage on the profits of our sales, that I would ask you freely to assess & eventually to cash directly from the publishers? I am asking for this favour because I feel that two publications at the same time, would ruin Cavafy's chances.

If you consent I could draw up a contract in due legal form and send it to you for your final approval.

If M. could also be induced to let me have some of his translations of the erotic stuff (the less lurid) that I feel incapable of rendering, it would

---

187 For the complications that arose from these conflicting translation plans, see Introduction, note 57.

be still better. However I feel that I could do without them and that C. can only gain by their omission.

As for my preface,[188] the enclosed passages are not quite final, but I am sending them all the same, because I would very much value your opinion, good or bad, owing to the vast experience that you have of an English public.

I sort of feel that the conclusion[189] is a bit too highly strung for the nerves of British readers and wants [. . .][190]

[George Valassopoulo]

81

[Dear Valassopoulo,]   [1944][191]

It is a great pleasure to hear from you again after all these years, and I do wish that [I] had not to write you a rather unsatisfactory reply. I will get the less agreeable part of my letter over first, and then turn to pleasanter matters.

Singopoulo has placed us all in a difficult position,[192] and I scarcely see the way out of it. After Cavafy's death, he asked me to find, with the help of Furness, an English translator and a publisher, and he told me that you had no intention of proceeding further with your translations. His wishes seemed quite clear, and I carried them out; Mavrocordato translated the whole of the poems, and Chatto and Windus would have been delighted

---

188 A draft of this preface (the "enclosed passages") exists in the Forster archive at King's College.

189 In his closing paragraph, Valassopoulo invites his "gentle" reader to share Cavafy's outlook, to celebrate life whether in the Greek islands, the fiords of Norway, "perusing, the while, on the deck of your ship, in the brilliancy of an arctic midnight, a volume of Ibsen, E. M. Forster, or of our poet . . . ."

190 The final page of this letter is missing.

191 This unfinished letter exists in typescript but is unsigned and undated. Most likely it was written in either February or March 1944.

192 See Introduction, note 58 regarding Singopoulo's "new scheme."

to publish that. Singopoulo to send sum of money to the Translator and the publisher (£100 to each, I think, though I have not a note on this), and a contract between the publishers and himself was to be drawn up. But he did not send the money,[193] nor did he answer my letters, although I wrote constantly, and even had my letters translated into French, to meet his convenience.

I do not blame him for this — I believe that he had certain difficulties at the time which prevented him from going forward with his scheme[194] — but you will appreciate what a difficult situation has been created when he came forward to day with a totally new scheme. I heard from him a couple of weeks ago, and did not know how to reply to his letter without offending him: so I am particularly glad to hear from you, for you and I are old friends, and I can write more freely without fear of misunderstanding. Singopoulo is under no obligation to me, nor to the publishers, and in neither of these cases does any problem arise. But I do think that he is under obligation to Mavrocordato, and that the new plan cannot go forward, until he has written to him, and (I suggest) made some offer of compensation to him. I cannot undertake this myself, nor can I do anything about conciliating the claims of the two translations, nor about the contract.

[. . .]

[EM Forster]

82

20/11/46

The Hogarth Press
40-42 William IV Street

---

193 A check from Barclay's Bank for £50 pounds was sent by Singopoulo to Leonard Woolf at the Hogarth Press on 12 October 1946 "against the £100 required for translating fees." (Cavafy Archive, Athens).

194 Singopoulo complains to Forster in a letter dated 11 January 1944 of health and business setbacks that impacted his support for the projected Cavafy translation (Cavafy Archive, Athens).

Dear Morgan,

I have just had one of the great triumphs of my life. I have received from Singopoulo a signed agreement giving me the right to publish Cavafy in Mavro's translation. I shall do it complete. The triumph would be complete if you would write an introduction to it.[195] Would you?

Yours,
Leonard Woolf

83

Aug 25
1951

KING'S COLLEGE,
CAMBRIDGE.

Dear Valassopoulo

What a pleasure to hear from you after all these years! and I am so glad you think well of the Mavrogordato[196] translations. I <u>much</u> prefer yours, but he has done a sound and conscientious piece of work, and (speaking personally) I am glad he translated all the poems. It would never have done to present the erotic poems alone, but they have their place in the complete body of the work and (as far as I know) Cavafy never sought to wi with withdraw them.

I am not quite sure from your letter whether you have seen my article on the book in <u>The Listener</u>.[197] If you haven't, I will send you a copy. The article was also broadcast in Greek in the Overseas Service of the B.B.C., and it will be reprinted in my forthcoming book of essays,[198] Oct. It was just in time to get in.

---

195 On Forster's tarrying with his introduction, see Introduction, p. 19.
196 John Mavrogordato's edition of *The Poems of C.P. Cavafy* (Hogarth Press) was finally published in 1951 following a lengthy delay.
197 Forster's review "In the rue Lepsius" appeared in *The Listener* (5 July 1951).
198 *Two Cheers for Democracy* was published in November 1951 by Edward Arnold.

Thank you for your good wishes about my Honorary Fellowship here.[199] It gave me great pleasure, especially since a room in college is attached. I am on A staircase — the first on the left as you come in, if you can remember the far-off scene. I have also got a Litt. D. from the University. So I feel well established in the academic scene, and I have also a little flat in London.[200] I keep pretty busy. Besides ~~the collected~~ collecting the essays, I have been helping to write a libretto for an opera by Benjamin Britten,[201] whose name you may know. He is the chief of our younger composers. The opera is based on a story of Herman Melville's called 'Billy Budd' and the first performance is at Covent Garden on Dec 1st. We are all getting very excited about it. It is a large scale work — chorus of nearly 80 — and the action takes place on a British Man of War at the end of the 18th century.

Now that I have told you my news I hope you will write again and tell me yours. You say you are retired. I trust that you keep good health and that you will be publishing your Cavafy translations.

Yours very sincerely
EM Forster

Please give my kind remembrances to Singopoulo.

84

KING'S COLL. CAMB.   Dec 30th
                                                                        1955

My dear Valassopoulo,

It was very pleasant to get a letter from you, also strange, for I had been thinking definitely about you a few days previously, and wondering

---

199 Forster received an honorary doctorate from Cambridge University in June 1950.
200 Forster had a London *pied-à-terre* at 9 Arlington Park Mansions, Sutton Lane, Chiswick.
201 Benjamin Britten (1913–1976), British composer for whom Forster, in collaboration with Eric Crozier, wrote the libretto of *Billy Budd*.

how you were. —Certainly there was a reason why I should think of you, to which I will presently come: but it was strange all the same.

I am looking forward to the French Cavafy,[202] which I should find at Cambridge when I return there next week. Good news about the German.[203] And even in England he won't be forgotten. A series of undergraduates keep reading and admiring him, and I get them to compare your translations, where they exist, with Mavrogordato's, and all agree that yours have caught something which his miss. Poor M! Quite meritorious, but so dead.

You mention my <u>Abinger Harvest</u>. Have you come across the companion volume, <u>Two Cheers for Democracy</u>, which came out a few years back and contains my article on the poems? The article I think I sent you at the time. If you can't get hold of the volume, and would care to possess a copy, I would be happy to send you one. But you will have to write me a second letter in this case!

You only <u>indicate</u> your news. I gather incidentally that you are the father of a family.[204] [I] wish you all happiness, and should welcome further details. I still live at King's, now have two large rooms there instead of one, and am really very comfortable. I also keep my small flat down in Chiswick.[205] My health is good considering my age, and much better than it was a few years ago. I had a wonderful fortnight's drive in France during the autumn—including the Lascaux Cave, the gorges of the Tarn, Provence and Burgundy. England since then has seemed cramped and provincial. So all being well I shall quit its shores again at the end of March and go for a cruise in the Greek Islands. —This brings me back to the beginning of the letter, to which kindly refer! Thinking of the tour made me think of Greek friends, and of you. We go from Venice to Itea, Athens one day only, then various islands down to Crete and Rhodes, back to the

---

202 Forster most likely refers to Marguerite Yourcenar's translation of sixteen Cavafy poems for *La Table ronde* (Paris, 1954).
203 A German translation of Cavafy by Helmut von den Steinen, *Gedichte des Konstantin Kavafis*, was published in Berlin in 1953.
204 George Valassopoulo and his wife Margherita had two children, Paul and Irene.
205 See letter 83, note 200.

mainland, through the canal again to Corfu, then Venice. All very touristy but I don't see how else I can go. My last visit was in 1903.

I wonder whether Cyprus[206] will lead to cancellation. I am much upset over the situation there. I am sure that Gt Britain ought to have cleared out.

Sheppard[207] (after whom you enquire) retired from being Provost some months back, and was succeeded by Stephen Glanville the Egyptologist, an ~~excellent~~ excellent choice. If you ever come across him in Egypt, do get into touch. He has not been many years in King's—an Oxford man. S. (Sir John Sheppard) had an operation lately, but has made vigourous recovery and is to be frank a bit of a nuisance. (All old men develop into nuisances, I'm afraid, and one never knows which type of nuisance one is). Sheppard also goes on a Hellenic Cruise, but on a smarter one than ours, and he will lecture.

You will remember Robin Furness, and you will be sorry to hear that he died some months ago.

I have just finished writing a long book[208]—a life of a great aunt, compiled out of family papers. It comes out in England and America during the spring. Now I have to make an index to it, which means much work.

With all good wishes for 1956:

Yours very sincerely

Morgan Forster

Remember me to anyone who may remember me, please.

85

KING'S COLL., CAMB.   March 22
                                                         1956

My dear Valassopoulo,

---

206 In April 1955, anti-British riots broke out in Cyprus demanding unification with Greece.

207 John Tresidder Sheppard, Provost of King's College, Cambridge.

208 *Marianne Thornton: A Domestic Biography* (1956).

I am glad my Two Cheers . . .[209] reached you, and M's French translation of Cavafy[210] safely reached me, and I think it looks very good.

It seems that we do go to the Aegean next week.[211] I go with mixed feelings. I don't expect to encounter danger or even discomfort, but there can be no friendliness such as I encountered half a century ago.—I may send you a p.c. [postcard] if I see a nice one!

With all good wishes, and it has been very nice getting into touch with you again,

Yours v. sincerely
EM Forster

Sheppard[212] much pleased with your message. He too is attempting a Hellenic Cruise, but not on the same boat.

86

K[ing's] C[ollege,] C[ambridge]
July 25 1958

Dear George [Savidis][213]

I have just finished, with a good deal of excitement and occasional doubts, Marguerite Yourcenar's "Cavafy".[214] I don't like the translation, the preface has not the authoritative tone I found in her "Hadrian", and the Parisian interventions of Mallarmé, Utrillo &[ct], rather jar. But she says many good things, and when I have written to you I must try to write

---

209 *Two Cheers for Democracy* (1951).
210 Marguerite Yourcenar (see letter 84, note 202).
211 Forster went on a Hellenic Society tour of Greece and Turkey. He would write an article about this trip, "Tourism v. Thuggism," for *The Listener* (17 January, 1957) in which he laments that "Tourism—an ugly word for an ugly thing— . . . spreads vulgarity."
212 See letter 84, note 207.
213 George Savidis (1929–1995), Greek professor, was the pre-eminent Cavafy scholar whose critical and archival work laid the groundwork for all future work on the poet. For his central role in preserving the Forster–Cavafy letters, see Introduction, p. 20.
214 Marguerite Yourcenar's *Présentation critique de Constantin Cavafy suivie d'une traduction des Poèmes par M. Yourcenar et Constantin Dimaras* was published by Gallimard in 1958.

to her and tell her so. (Not but what she is likely to know about them already.) One of them is her discovery that Cavafy is, and always potentially was, an <u>old</u> poet, another her suggestion that his own erotic life may never have been continuous or strong. And she does bring out, though without stating it, his triumph—a triumph that has nothing to do with success. Sick of getting through my final years by British jokiness, I have had a timely reminder of another method.

I turned from her translation to Wooden cordato's, which is reliable rather than inspired. Then I tried to turn to Cavafy himself, but where can I have put him?

I heard from someone, Noel[215] I think, that you might be allowed to see the unpublished papers. I should be interested in them and in anything about him, but, with his type of mind, I should doubt whether he had anything to conceal beyond names places and dates. How very proud I am, George, that I ever got to know him; it is certainly one of my 'triumphs'. R. A. Furness took me to see him in 1916–17.

                Above is a letter from
                Morgan

---

215 Noël Gilroy Annan, Provost of King's College.

Cavafy Anthology

Translated by
George Valassopoulo

Edited by
Katerina Ghika and Peter Jeffreys

An Alexandrian Poet: C.P. Cavafy

by G.A. Valassopoulo

Mr. C.P. Cavafy is certainly the most original of modern Greek poets and would be better known to the reading public were it not for his modesty and his firm decision to reserve his poems for private circulation only.

Cavafy was born and has lived almost all his life in Alexandria, a city of which the least that can be said is, that it is not inspiring.

Badly built on a narrow strip of coast, between the Mediterranean and Lake Mariout, without even the semblance of a plan, with hardly any remains of her historic past, without the glamour of the Moslem East, lacking traditions, lacking proper sanitation, Alexandria is merely a dumping-ground for all the races of the East and the West that meet here, without blending.

The city of the present day fully justifies the Emperor Hadrian's well-known remark concerning the Alexandrians, that, whether they are Christians, Jews or Hellenes, they have only one God whom they worship with the utmost zeal, and that is wealth.

The life of the modern City centres almost entirely round the "Bourse" (Cotton Exchange) where absurd speculations prevail and fortunes are made or lost in a few days.

Cotton is also staunchly seconded by such minor products as onions, eggs and rice.

But it must not be thought that any comparison is possible, to-day, with the old Greek City, because even in its decline, ancient Alexandria could be justly proud of Philo and Plotinus, Porphyry and Hypatia.

However we have Cavafy!

The poet, it is true, owes nothing to the modern City or his present surroundings.

Still, the mere fact that poetry, and poetry of a high order, is possible in such an uncongenial spot, is a matter of some surprise to his friends.

The poet's world is ancient Alexandria, the luxury or the vanity of her rulers, Cleopatra and her desperate struggle with Rome, the rise and later the establishment of Christianity, the Hellenistic kingdom of Seleucus and Antiochus, Apollonius of Tyana, Greek culture in the wild confines of the Hellenic world, etc., etc.

Such is Cavafy's world, with occasional incursions into Classical Greece and still fewer digressions to Byzantium.

Cavafy's attitude is that of an historian more than of a poet. He is at great pains to be, as far as possible, historically correct. He is almost always an impartial observer of history with, perhaps one exception—his zeal for the Christian and more especially the Orthodox Church to which he belongs.

We are apt to associate poetry with a spirit of antagonism towards established ideas and established creeds and such an attitude would have been natural in a Greek poet who records the tragic fate of the Hellenic world at the hands of the Romans first, and of the Christians afterwards.

But Cavafy is unmoved.

There is, in his poems, none of the fiery indignation of Leconte de Lisle's "Hypatia."

On the contrary, he plays havoc with such commanding figures as Julian, the so-called Apostate.

Cavafy sneers at the great Emperor, at his beard, his awkward manners, his "ludicrous" attempt to reform the Pagan faith.

Impolitic, untimely, desperate, perhaps, but surely not "ludicrous."

Cavafy's irony is his dominant trait, sometimes forcibly expressed as in the poem "When Julian Observed Much Lukewarmness", sometimes only faintly outlined.

But Cavafy is no revolutionary.

The lightness of his touch, the art with which a deep hidden meaning or a vein of philosophic resignation appears at the end of a poem which otherwise may seem devoid of interest, the reality which he imparts even to his shortest poems and the life he brings into a period which is only too often treated in a classical stereotyped manner, are the mark of a poet whose originality is undoubted and who deserves to be better known outside his native country.

[. . .]

G.A. Valassopoulo
Alexandria, June 30, 1931

(Originally published in *Échanges* 5 December 1931)

Alexandrian Kings

An Alexandrian crowd collected
to see the sons of Cleopatra,
Caesarion and his little brothers
Alexander and Ptolemy, who for the first
time were brought to the Gymnasium,
there to be crowned as kings
amidst a splendid display of troops.

Alexander they named king
of Armenia, of Media, and of the Parthians.
Ptolemy they named king
of Cilicia, of Syria, and Phoenicia.
Caesarion stood a little in front,
clad in silk the colour of roses,
with a bunch of hyacinths at his breast.
His belt was a double line of sapphires and amethysts,
his sandals were bound with white ribbons
embroidered with rosy pearls.
Him they acclaimed more than the small ones.
Him they named "King of Kings!"

The Alexandrians knew perfectly well
that all this was words and empty pomp.

But the day was warm and exquisite,
the sky clear and blue,
the Gymnasium of Alexandria a triumph of art,
the courtiers' apparel magnificent,
Caesarion full of grace and beauty
(son of Cleopatra, blood of the Lagidae!),
and the Alexandrians ran to see the show

and grew enthusiastic, and applauded
in Greek, in Egyptian, and some in Hebrew,
bewitched with the beautiful spectacle,
though they knew perfectly well how worthless,
what empty words, were these king-makings.

(Published in *Pharos and Pharillon*, 1923)

Anna Comnena

In her preamble to the *Alexiad*
Anna Comnena laments her widowhood.

Her soul is in a turmoil. "And"
she tells us "torrents of tears fill
my eyes . . . Alas, the storms" of her life
"alas, the revolutions." Her grief consumes her
"to the bone and the marrow, and to rending of her soul".

But the truth seems to be that the ambitious woman
knew only of one deep sorrow,
the haughty Greek woman had only one great anguish, —
though she may not confess it, —
that, for all her dexterity, she had not succeeded
in obtaining the crown, but it was snatched,
almost out of her hands, by the daring John.

(Unpublished draft from the Cavafy Archive)

Aristobulos

The palace weeps, the king weeps,
King Herod laments disconsolate,
all the city weeps for Aristobulos
who thus unjustly and by chance was drowned
while playing with his friends in the water.

And when they hear of it in other parts,
when the news is spread up there in Syria
of the Hellenes also many will grieve;
those who are poets and sculptors will mourn,
because the fame of Aristobulos had come to them,
for which of their visions of a youthful form ever
had arrived at so much beauty as was this boy's?
With what statue of a god was Antioch
ever endowed like to this child of Israel?

The First Princess laments and weeps;
his mother the greatest of the Jewesses.
Alexandra laments and weeps for the calamity. —
But when she is alone her grief changes.
She groans; she rages; she abuses; she casts imprecations.
How she was mocked! How she was cheated!
How after all was their end attained!
They have ruined the house of the Asamonians.
How did he accomplish it, the criminal king,
the treacherous, the bad, the worthless,
how did he accomplish it? What an underground plot,
that even Marianne did not perceive anything.
Had Marianne noticed, if only she had suspected,
she would have found a means of saving her brother;
After all she is a queen, she would have done something.

How triumphant they must be now and secretly they must rejoice
those worthless women, Kypros and Salome;
those vulgar women Kypros and Salome.
And she is powerless, she is forced
to pretend that she believes their lies;
And she cannot go to the people.
She cannot go out and shout to the Jews,
to tell them, to tell them how
the murder was committed.

(Unpublished draft from King's College, Cambridge)

Caesarion

Partly in order to make sure of a date,
and partly also to while away the time,
last night, I took up and read
a collection of inscriptions of Ptolemis.
Unlimited praise and flattery are meted
to all alike. They are all splendid,
famous, powerful and bounteous;
All their enterprises are most wise.
If you look for the women of that lineage
they also, the Berenices and the Cleopatras, are admirable.

When I made sure of the epoch
I would have put aside the book, were it not
for a small and unimportant reference to king Caesarion
which attracted my attention . . .

Ah! you came to me with your undefined
charm. History has consecrated
but a few lines to you,
and thus, I am free to fashion you in my mind.
I fancied you beautiful and sensitive.
My art lends to your countenance
a dreamy and engaging comeliness.
And so real was your image,
that late last night, when my lamp
was waning—I allowed it to go out—
I thought that you came into my room;
meseemed you stood in front of me;
such as you were in captive Alexandria
pale and tired, ideal in your grief,

hoping yet for mercy from the knaves
—who whispered: "Beware of many Caesars".

(Unpublished draft from King's College, Cambridge)

Come Back

Come back often and take me,
beloved sensation come back and take me—
when awakes the body's memory,
and an old desire again courses through my blood;
when the lips and the skin remember,
and the hands feel as though they were touching again.

Come back often, at night, and take me,
when the lips and the skin remember . . .

(Unpublished draft from King's College, Cambridge)

Dangerous Thoughts

Said Myrtias (a Syrian student
at Alexandria; in the reign of Augustus
Constans and Augustus Constantius;
partly a pagan and partly Christianizing)
"Fortified as I shall be by theory and study
I shall not, like the timorous, stand in fear of my passions.
I shall deliver my body to pleasures,
to the joys of which one dreams,
to the boldest erotic desires,
to the lustful promptings of the flesh,
without any fear, because whenever I wish—
and I shall have the will fortified
as I shall be by theory and study—
whenever the crisis comes I shall regain
a spirit ascetic as before".

(Unpublished draft from the Cavafy Archive)

Darius

The poet Phernazes is at work
upon an important passage in his epic poem;
how the Kingdom of Persia
is secured by Darius, son of Hystaspes
(from whom is descended our glorious king
Mithradates Dionysus Eupator).
The passage is philosophic. He has to describe
the feelings that animated Darius:
"arrogance" perhaps and "exultation"; or no—
more probably a sense of the vanity of human greatness.
The poet is meditating deeply on his theme.

Running in, his servant interrupts him,
and brings a most serious piece of news.
The war with the Romans has begun.
Our army in full force has crossed the frontier.

The poet is speechless. What a misfortune!
How will our glorious king
Mithradates Dionysus Eupator
find time to listen to Greek poetry now?
In the middle of a war—Greek poetry, indeed!

Phernazes is in despair. Alas, alas!
His "Darius" was certain to bring him fame
and silence once for all those envious detractors.
What a set-back, what a set-back to his plans!

Were it only a set-back, no matter,
but shall we be quite safe at Amisus?
The city walls are none of the strongest,

the Romans are most terrible enemies.
Can we hold our own against them,
we Cappadocians? Is it likely?
Can we make a stand against the legions?
Help! Help! O ye Great Gods, protectors of Asia, defend us.

Yet through all his distress and anxiety
the poetic obsession still comes and goes;
surely "arrogance" and "exultation" are more probable;
yes, "arrogance" and "exultation" were the feelings that animated Darius.

(Published in *The Nation & the Athenaeum* 34.1, 6 October 1923)

Demaratus

A subject, "the character of Demaratus"
was suggested to the young sophist, in conversation,
by Porphyry and was treated by him thus:
(he intended, later, to develop the subject, in rhetoric).

"He was courtier, first, to king Darius,
and afterwards, to king Xerxes;
and now, with Xerxes and his host,
there will be justice for Demaratus".

"He was victim of a grievious wrong.
He *was* son of Ariston. His enemies
bribed the Oracle shamelessly.
They took, from him, his kingdom
and not content with this,
when he submitted and bravely
resolved to remain a simple citizen,
they needs must insult him before the people,
they needs must humiliate him, in public, at the festival".

"So he serves Xerxes with great zeal.
With the great Persian host
he too, shall go back to Sparta;
And a king again, he shall hasten
To drive out ignominiously
that intriguer, Leotychidas".

"And his days wax full of care;
with deep counsel to the Persians
how to achieve the conquest of Greece".

"Many cares, much thought, and that is why
Demaratus' days are so irksome;
Many cares, much thought, and that is why
Demaratus has not a moment of joy;
for that is no joy Demaratus feels
(it is not; he will never admit it;
how can he call it joy? His ill-fortune culminates)
when the facts tell him plainly
that the Greeks will be the victors".

(Unpublished draft from King's College, Cambridge)

Demetrius Soter (B.C. 162–150)

All his plans have failed!

He thought he could accomplish great deeds,
that he would end the humiliation that oppressed
his country from the time of the battle of Magnesia.
Syria would become a powerful state again—
with her armies, with her fleets,
with her strong fortresses, with her riches.

At Rome, he suffered, he was embittered
when he noticed in conversation with his friends,
the young men of the noble houses,—
in spite of all the courtesy and the tact
which they showed to him, the son
of king Seleucus Philopator—
when he noticed that there was always
a veiled disesteem for the Hellenistic dynasties,
which had declined, which were not for serious things,
which were wholly unsuited for the government of nations.
Indignant, he used to draw aside, and vow
that things would not be as they thought;
he, at least, had a will;
he would struggle, he would achieve, he would uphold.

If only he could find his way to the East,
if he could effect his escape from Italy—
he would impart to the people
all the strength that he carried
in his soul, all the enthusiasm.

Could he but find himself in Syria!

He had left his country so young
that he remembered only faintly its features.
But it was always present in his thoughts
as something sacred to be approached with reverence,
as a picture of a most beautiful land, as a mirage
of Greek cities and harbours. —

And now?
     Now is despair and lamentation.
The boys at Rome were right.
It is not possible to sustain the dynasties
that arose from the Macedonian conquest.

But it does not matter:
he fought as long as he could.
And in his black despair
he reckons only one thing
with pride: that even in his misfortune
he shows the same indomitable courage before all the world.

For the rest—it was a dream and vain endeavour.
This Syria—she almost seems not to be his country,
she is the land of Heraclides and of Bala.

(Unpublished draft from the Cavafy Archive)

Did He Die?

"Where did the Sage withdraw, where did he disappear?
After his many miracles,
after the fame of his teaching
had spread among a number of nations,
he suddenly hid himself, and none had heard
for certain, what had befallen him
(nor had anyone seen his grave).
It was rumoured by some that he died at Ephesus.
But Damis did not write of this; Damis did not write
anything about the death of Apollonius.
Others said that he vanished at Lindus.
Or is the tale true,
that he ascended to heaven, in Crete,
in the ancient sanctuary of Dictynna? —
But then, we have his wondrous,
supernatural apparition,
to a young student at Tyana. —
Perhaps, the day is not yet come for him to return,
to appear again to the world;
or perhaps, transfigured, he wanders
undetected among us. — But he will reappear
as he was, teaching the right word; and then he will
certainly restore the worship of our Gods,
and our beautiful Greek festivals".

Thus did one of the few pagans,
the very few that still remained,
muse in his lowly dwelling,
after reading Philostratus' book:
"Concerning Apollonius of Tyana".
He was withal, a faint-hearted man and of no consequence,

in public, he pretended that he was
a Christian and attended the church.
It was the time when the aged Justin
ruled with great piety;
and Alexandria, a God-fearing city,
abhorred the wicked idolaters.

(Published in *Échanges* 5 December 1931)

Envoys from Alexandria

For centuries such rich presents had not been seen at Delphi,
as those that had been sent by the two rival Kings
the brothers Ptolemy. But when the priests received them
they were embarrassed for their oracle.
They would need all their experience to compose it prudently;
which of the two, which of these great two
would it be less hazardous to displease.
And they held council at night secretly,
and they discussed the family differences of the Lagids.

But lo, the envoys reappear. They are bidding farewell.
They say that they are returning to Alexandria.
And they are asking for no oracle at all.
This is good tidings for the priests
(as a matter of course they are keeping the rich presents);
but they are also much surprised,
they do not understand what this sudden indifference means.
They do not know that on the previous day
serious news had come to the envoys. The oracle was given at Rome;
it was there that the Kingdom had been divided.

(Unpublished draft from the Cavafy Archive)

Far Away

I would this memory I could relate . . .
But somehow it is extinguished now . . . hardly anything remains —
for it lies far away, in my first years of youth.

A cheek, like one of jasmine . . .
That August evening—was it August? . . .
I remember but dimly, now, those eyes; they were, I think, blue . . .
Ah yes, blue; a sapphire blue.

(Unpublished draft from King's College, Cambridge)

For Ammones Who Died at the Age of 29 in the Year 610

Raphael, you are asked to compose a few verses
as an epitaph for the poet Ammones.
Something artistic and even. Assuredly, you can do it,
you are best suited for writing as is fitting
about our poet Ammones.

You will, of course, speak of his poems—
but you must also speak of his beauty,
his delicate beauty that we loved.

Your Greek is always elegant and harmonious.
But now we need all your skill.
Our sorrow and our love are passing into a foreign tongue.
You must pour your Egyptian feeling into the foreign tongue.

Raphael, your verses should be written in such a manner
that they contain, you know, something of our life,
that the rhythm and the phrasing show
that an Alexandrian is writing about an Alexandrian.

(Published in *The Criterion*, vol. 8, issue 30, September 1928)

Herodes Atticus

Ah what glory is this of Herodes Atticus!

Alexander of Seleucia, one of our good sophists,
on reaching Athens with the intention of delivering orations
found the town empty, because Herodes
was in the country. And all the young men
followed him there to hear him discourse.
So the sophist Alexander
wrote a letter to Herodes
and prayed him to send back the Greeks.
And the polite Herodes answered at once:
"I am coming together with the Greeks myself".

Many young men in Alexandria now,
in Antioch or in Berytus
(the coming orators whom Hellenism is preparing)
when they assemble, a chosen company, at banquets,
and converse sometimes about the fine art of the sophist,
and sometimes about the beautiful theme of their loves,
are suddenly absent-minded and silent.
They leave their cups untasted beside them,
and muse on Herodes' good fortune—
what other sophist was so honoured?—
According as he wishes and according as he does,
the Greeks (the Greeks!) follow him,
they neither criticise, nor discuss,
nor choose any more; they only follow.

(Unpublished draft from the Cavafy Archive)

[He is the Man]

An unknown Edesiene—a stranger in Antioch—
writes copiously. There, at length
the final lay is ended. This makes

eighty-three poems in all. But so much writing,
so much versification has fatigued the poet,
and so much attention to Grecian phraseology,
and now the least whit tires him.

One thought, however, at once rouses him from his prostration
the exquisite verse ["He is the Man"]
that Lucian heard in his sleep.

(Unpublished draft from King's College, Cambridge)

In a City of Asia Minor

The tidings of the issue of the naval battle of Actium,
were certainly unexpected.
However, we are not obliged to compose another document.
The name alone has to be altered. At the closing lines,
instead of the phrase: "Having delivered the Romans
from the wicked Octavius,
the counterfeit Caesar,"
we shall now say: "Having delivered the Romans
from the wicked Antony . . ."
All the text fits admirably.

"To the famous victor,
who is unequalled in every warlike enterprise,
most admirable in great affairs of State,
to Antony, for whose success,
the City offered prayers fervently,"
(here, as we said, we substitute, "Caesar"),
"deeming it, from Zeus, the greatest boon —
to the powerful protector of the Greeks,
who observes, with honour, Greek customs,
and is beloved in every Greek land,
who deserves signal praise,
whose actions are worthy of a lengthy record
couched in the Greek tongue, in prose and in verse;
in the Greek tongue which is the vehicle of fame,"
and so forth, and so forth. It all fits admirably.

(Published in *Échanges* 5 December 1931)

In a City of Osrhoene

From the tavern brawl they brought us
our friend Rhemon wounded, yesterday at about midnight.
The moon, coming through the window
that we had left wide open,
lit up his beautiful form lying on the bed.
We are a medley here; Syrians, Greeks, Armenians, Medes.
Such is Rhemon also. But yesterday
when the moon lit up his amorous face,
our thoughts went back to Plato's Charmides.

(Unpublished draft from King's College, Cambridge)

In the Church

I love the church—her standards,
her silver vessels, her candelabras,
her lights, her icons, her pulpit.

When I enter the Greek church:
with the fragrance of the incense,
with the liturgic chaunts,
with the majestic presences of the priests
and the solemn rhythm of all their movements—
they are magnificently robed in the holy vestments—
my thoughts go back to a great splendour of our race,
to our glorious Byzantine age.

(Unpublished draft from the Cavafy Archive)

In the Month of Athyr

It is hard to read . . . on the ancient stone.
"Lord Jesus Christ" . . . I make out the word "Soul".
"In the month of Athyr . . . Lucius fell asleep".
His age is mentioned . . . "He lived years . . . "—
The letters KZ show . . . that he fell asleep young.
In the damaged part I see the words . . . "Him . . . Alexandrian".
Then come three lines . . . much mutilated.
But I can read a few words . . . perhaps "our tears" and "sorrows".
And again: "Tears" . . . and: "for us his friends mourning".
I think Lucius . . . was much beloved.
In the month of Athyr . . . Lucius fell asleep . . .

(Published in *Pharos and Pharillon*, 1923)

Ionicon

Why did we break their statues,
why did we drive them from their temples?
The Gods died not through this.
Ionic land they love thee still.
Their souls still remember thee.
When an August morning dawns above thee
a throb of their life passes through the heaven.
And sometimes an etherial youthful form
half-seen, with eager tread,
passes over the hills.

(Published in *The Oxford Outlook* 26.6, February 1924)

Ithaca

When you start on the way to Ithaca,
wish that the way be long,
full of adventure, full of knowledge.
The Laestrygones and the Cyclopes
and angry Poseidon, do not fear:
such, on your way, you shall never meet
if your thoughts are lofty, if a noble
emotion touches your mind, your body.
The Laestrygones and the Cyclopes
and angry Poseidon you shall not meet
if you carry them not in your soul,
if your soul sets them not up before you.

Wish that the way be long,
that on many summer mornings,
with great pleasure, great delight,
you enter harbours for the first time seen;
that you stop at Phoenician marts,
and procure the goodly merchandise,
mother-of-pearl and corals, amber and ebony,
and sensual perfumes of all kinds,
plenty of sensual perfumes especially;
to wend your way to many Egyptian cities,
to learn and yet to learn from the wise.

Ever keep Ithaca in your mind,
your return thither is your goal.
But do not hasten at all your voyage,
better that it last for many years;
and full of years at length you anchor at your isle,

rich with all that you gained on the way;
do not expect Ithaca to give you riches.

Ithaca gave you your fair voyage.
Without her you would not have ventured on the way.
But she has no more to give you.

And if you find Ithaca a poor place, she has not mocked you.
You have become so wise, so full of experience,
that you should understand already what these Ithacas mean.

(Published in *The Criterion*, vol. 2, issue 8, July 1924)

Manuel Comnenus

On a dull September day,
Lord Manuel Comnenus the king,
felt that Death was near. The astrologers,
the court astrologers, who drew their pay, were prating,
that he would live for many years yet.
But while they talked, he recollects old habits of piety
and bids them bring him
holy garments from hermits' cells;
and garbed in these, he rejoices
in the modest demeanour of priest or friar.

Blest are they who have faith,
and like Lord Manuel the king they end their days,
clad in their faith most modestly.

(Unpublished draft from King's College, Cambridge)

Monotony

The one dull day another
as dull will follow. The same
things will occur and occur yet again,
the very same moments come to us and leave us.

Every month passes and brings another month.
Coming events can easily be foretold;
they are the same as yesterday's dull ones.
And to-morrow will almost seem not to be to-morrow.

(Published in *Échanges* 5 December 1931)

Nero's Span of Life

Nero was not disturbed when he heard
the oracle of the Delphic God which said:
"Beware of the years three and seventy".
He still had time to enjoy life.
His age was only thirty. The term assigned
by the God was ample
for him to guard against future dangers.

Now he is returning to Rome a little fatigued,
but exquisitely fatigued by his journey,
which was full of days of pleasure —
at the theatres, in the gardens, in the gymnasiums . . .
The evenings in the Achaean cities . . .
Above all the lovely naked bodies . . .

So much for Nero. And in Spain, Galba
is secretly recruiting and training his forces,
the old man, of seventy-three.

(Unpublished draft from the Cavafy Archive)

THE TOMB OF LANÈS

The Lanès ~~that~~ whom you loved is not here, Marcus, remain

in the tomb near which you come and weep, and ~~stand~~
and hours.
for hours ~~at end.~~ You keep the Lanès ~~that~~ whom you loved

nearer ~~to you, in your house,~~ when you confine yourself in your house

Which somehow has retained what ~~thing of his meri~~
~~was~~ of value in him ~~loved.~~
which somehow has retained what
you ~~most~~ loved

the ~~famous~~ Cyrenean ~~painter from the~~ consul's palace,

~~and he with an artist's guile~~
shrewd
and ~~when he saw your friend, wished to persuade~~ you
m
that he ~~must~~ represent him as Hyacinthus
so
(~~that~~ his picture would become more famous).

But Lanès would not lend his beauty thus;
resisting
and, firmly ~~decided,~~ he told the painter

to represent not Hyacinthus, not anyone else,

but Lanès, son of Rametichus, ~~an~~ Alexandrian.

                              C.P.CAVAFY

(Translated by G.Valassopoulo).

has cunningly he tried to persuade you
when he saw your friend

13. Typescript of Valassopoulo's translation of "The Tomb of Lanès," with Cavafy's handwritten corrections.

15. Page from *The Oxford Outlook*, 1924.

16. Cover of *Échanges*, December 1931.

14. Literary advertisements from *The Spectator*, July 1924. "Sic Semper" ("thus ever") was written in by Forster.

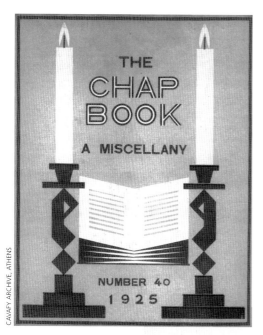

CONTENTS

5

17. Cover and table of contents from *The Chapbook*, 1925.

18. Postcard from Forster to Valassopoulo, 1923.

8 . 8 . 29

My dear Forster,

Your letter of the 8th July (which I received yesterday) has made me happy.

I have no intention of leaving Alexandria this year; so I shall have the great satisfaction of seeing you again. I am looking forward to it. Immediately you arrive in Alexandria, let me know, please.

I am very glad at the news.

Ever yours,

C. P. Cavafy

19. Cavafy's letter to Forster, 8 August 1929.

THE CRITERION
A QUARTERLY REVIEW

Published by R. Cobden-Sanderson,
17 Thavies Inn, London, E.C.1.

Telephone: Holborn 1950

September 8th 1924.

Received from R.Cobden-Sanderson (on behalf of the
Proprietor) the sum of £1 -10- 0 (one pound, ten
shillings) in payment for contribution "I T H A C A"
to The Criterion No.8. July 1924.

C.P.Cavafy Esq.,
c/o T.S. Eliot Esq.,
9 Clarence Gate Gardens,
N.W.1.

20. Letter of payment from
The Criterion, 8 July 1924.

The Hogarth Press

Memorandum of agreement made this
13th day of November 1925 between C.P.Cavafy
Esq. of 10 Rue Lepsius, alexandria, Egypt
(hereinafter termed the Author) of the one
part and the Hogarth Press, 52 Tavistock
Square, London W.C.1 (hereinafter termed
the Publishers) of the other part. Whereby it
is mutually agreed between the parties
hereto for themselves and their respective
executors, administrators and assigns (or
successors, as the case may be), as follows: —

1. The publishers shall at their own risk
and expense produce and publish "Poems" by
the Author.

2. The Author guarantee to the Publishers

21. Cavafy's handwritten copy of the Hogarth Press contract,
1925.

22. The Reform Club, London.

23. Forster's home, "West Hackhurst," in Abinger Hammer, Dorking.

24. King's College, Cambridge, Forster's residence from 1946 to 1970.

25. George Savidis as a student at King's College, Cambridge, circa 1952.

Of the Jews (50 A.D.)

Ianthes, son of Antonius, was beautiful like Endymion;
a painter and a poet, a runner and a thrower of the disc;
of a family with a leaning for the Synagogue.

"My noblest days are those
on which I forego the pursuit of aesthetic impressions,
when I abandon the beautiful, yet hard, Greek life
with its dominant attachment
to perfectly shapen and corruptible white limbs.
And I become, what I would wish
always to remain, a son of the Jews, of the holy Jews".

Very earnest, this assertion,
"always to remain a son of the Jews, of the holy Jews".

But he did not remain as such at all.
The Hedonism and the Art of Alexandria
had in him a devoted son.

(Unpublished draft from the Cavafy Archive)

One of Their Gods

When one of them used to pass by the market-place
of Seleucia, about the time of nightfall,
a tall young man of perfect beauty,
with the joy of immortality in his eyes
and perfumed black hair,
the people used to watch him
and ask one another whether they knew him,
whether he was a Syrian Greek or a stranger. But some
who looked with greater attention
understood and made way;
and while he disappeared under the archways
among the evening lights and the shadows
on his way to the place that lives only at night
with orgies and drunkenness
and every kind of lust and debauchery,
they wondered which of Them it was
and for what unavowed pleasure
he had come down to the streets of Seleucia
from the Sacred and Hallowed Dwellings.

(Published in *The Chapbook* 40, 1925)

Orophernes

He who on the tetradrachm
appears to be smiling,
with a delicate beautiful face,
is Orophernes, son of Ariarathes.

A child still, he was exiled from Cappadocia,
from the great ancestral palace,
and he was sent to grow up
in Ionia, and to be forgotten among strangers.

In the exquisite Ionian nights
fearless and in genuine Greek fashion
he gained the full knowledge of pleasure.
In his heart he still remained an Asiatic,
but in his manners and his speech he was a Greek;
he wore rich turquoises, he was dressed in the Greek garb,
and among the handsome young men of Ionia
he was the most handsome.

Later, when the Syrians invaded Cappadocia
and made him king,
he clung to the throne
to enjoy every day in a different manner,
to amass rapaciously gold and silver
and to rejoice and boast
watching the glitter of his hoarded riches.

The Cappadocians speedily drove him out;
and he drifted to Syria, to idleness
and pleasures in the palace of Demetrius.

But one day unusual thoughts
interrupted his gross idleness;
he remembered that through his mother Antiochis,
and through his ancestress Stratonice
he too had a claim on the crown of Syria,
that he was almost a Seleucid.
For a short time he emerged from debauchery and drunkenness;
feebly and half-dazed he tried to intrigue,
to do something, to plan something;
and he failed most ignominiously.

His end may have been told somewhere,
but the record is lost; or perhaps History passed it by,
and, very rightly, did not condescend
to record such a paltry subject.

He who on the tetradrachm
has left some of the charm of his comely youth,
some lights of his poetic beauty,
an artistic remembrance of an Ionian youth,
is Orophernes, son of Ariarathes.

(Unpublished draft from the Cavafy Archive)

So That They Come . . .

One candle is enough.   Its faint light
is better suited,   it will have more charm
when the Shadows come,   the Shadows of Love.

One candle is enough.   The room tonight
should not have too much light.   As in a dream
and in a trance,   and in the faint light—
as in a dream   I shall be rapt in contemplation
so that the Shadows come,   the Shadows of Love.

(Unpublished draft from King's College, Cambridge)

The City

You said: "I shall go to some other land, I shall go to some other sea.
Another city there must be, better than this.
My every effort here is a sentence of condemnation against me,
and my heart—like a corpse—lies buried.
How long shall my mind remain smothered in this blight?
Wherever I turn my eye, wherever I look,
I see the black ruins of my life
where I spent and spoiled and ruined so many years".

Fresh lands you shall not find, you shall not find other seas.
The city shall ever follow you.
In streets you shall wander that are the same streets and
    grow old in quarters that are the same
and among these very same houses you shall turn grey.
You shall always be returning to the city. Hope not;
there is no ship to take you to other lands, there is no road.
You have so spoiled your life here in this tiny corner
that you have ruined it in all the world.

(Published in *The Nation & The Athenaeum*, vol. 35, issue 6, 5 April 1924)

The Displeasure of the Seleucid

Demetrius the Seleucid was displeased
when he heard that a Ptolemy
had come to Rome in such an evil plight;
accompanied by three or four servants only,
meanly dressed and on foot. Their races would thus
become a laughing stock and a byword
at Rome. The Seleucid knew quite well
that they were really a kind of dependant
of the Romans; that it was the Romans who gave them,
and who deprived them of, their thrones
at will, arbitrarily.
But at least in their appearance
they should retain some kind of splendour;
they should not forget that they were still kings,
that they still were called (alas!) kings.

That is why the Seleucid Demetrius was upset;
and he hastened to offer Ptolemy
purple robes, a fine diadem,
costly jewels, numerous attendants,
and most expensive horses,
so that he appear at Rome with proper decorum,
like an Alexandrian Greek monarch.

But the Lagid, who had come to beg,
knew better, and he refused all the offers;
he had no use at all for this finery.
He entered Rome in humble manner, and meanly dressed,
and stopped at the house of a modest artist.
And then he attended the Senate,

like a poor man, like a beggar,
thus to beg with greater effect.

(Unpublished draft from the Cavafy Archive)

The End

We are consumed with fear and suspicion,
and with distracted mind and frightened glances
we make plans in order to escape the certain
danger that menaces us so desperately.
But we are mistaken, this danger is not in our path;
the messages were false
or then, we did not hear, or did not understand them rightly.
Another undreamed of calamity
falls on us, sudden and impetuous,
and unprepared—there is no time now—overwhelms us.

(Published in *Échanges* 5 December 1931)

The God Abandons Antony

When at the hour of midnight
an invisible choir is suddenly heard passing
with exquisite music, with voices—
Do not lament your fortune that at last subsides,
your life's work that has failed, your schemes that have proved illusions.
But like a man prepared, like a brave man,
bid farewell to her, to Alexandria who is departing.
Above all, do not delude yourself, do not say that it is a dream,
that your ear was mistaken.
Do not condescend to such empty hopes.
Like a man for long prepared, like a brave man,
like the man who was worthy of such a city,
go to the window firmly,
and listen with emotion
but not with the prayers and complaints of the coward
(Ah! supreme rapture!)
listen to the notes, to the exquisite instruments of the mystic choir,
and bid farewell to her, to Alexandria whom you are losing.

(Published in *Pharos and Pharillon*, 1923)

The Ides of March

Beware, my soul, of passing greatness,
and conquer thy love of glory,
if thou canst not, follow thine ambition hesitatingly
and on thy guard. The higher thou wingest
the more thou shouldst probe and take heed.

And when thou comest, Caesar, to the pinnacle of greatness,
and assumest the dignity of so great a man,
then especially beware, when thou comest into the street,
a great man conspicuous among thy retinue;
if from the crowd were to approach thee
one Artemidorus, bearing a letter,
and saying hurriedly: "Read it forthwith
for it contains great tidings concerning thee,"
do not fail to pause; do not fail to adjourn
every conversation, every business; do not fail
to dismiss all those who greet thee and bend the knee
(thou canst see them anon); let even the Senate
await thee, and take heed at once
of the weighty tidings of Artemidorus.

(Published in *The Oxford Outlook* 26.6, February 1924)

The Meaning

The years of my youth, my life of pleasure—
how clearly now do I realise their meaning.

Needless, vain, is repentance . . .

But I did not realise the meaning then.

In the unrestrained life of my youth
the law of my poetry was taking shape
the scope of my art was being planned.

That is why my repentance was never steadfast
and my resolve to control myself and to alter
lasted a fortnight at most.

(Unpublished draft from King's College, Cambridge)

The Sea of a Morning

Here let me stand. Let me too look at Nature a little,
the radiant blue of the morning sea,
the cloudless sky and the yellow beach;
all beautiful and flooded with light.

Here let me stand. And let me deceive myself into thinking that I saw
    them—
(I really did see them one moment, when first I came)
—that I am not seeing, even here, my fancies,
my memories, my visions of voluptuousness.

(Published in *The Athenaeum* 9 May 1919)

The Tomb of Eurion

In this ornate monument,
built all of syenite stone,
and strewn with many violets and many lilies,
is buried fair Eurion.
A son of Alexandria, twenty-five years old.
Through his father he was of old Macedonian stock;
his mother's lineage came from Alabarchae.
He was a pupil of Aristoclitus in philosophy,
of Parus in rhetoric. He composed a history
of the Arsinoite nome. This, at least, will remain.
But we have lost something more valuable—his features,
which were as a semblance of Apollo.

(Unpublished draft from King's College, Cambridge)

The Tomb of Ignatius

Here no longer am I Cleon who was famous
in Alexandria (where people are not prone to admire)
for my rich houses, for my gardens,
for my horses and for my chariots,
for the jewels and for the silk robes that I wore.
Begone; here no longer am I that Cleon;
let his twenty-eight years be obliterated.
I am Ignatius the deacon
who came late, very late, to contrition; but even so
I lived ten happy months
in the peace and in the safe keeping of Christ.

(Unpublished draft from the Cavafy Archive)

The Tomb of Lanes [I]

The Lanes that you loved is not here, Marcus,
in the tomb near which you come and weep, and stand
for hours on end. You keep the Lanes that you loved
nearer to you, in your house, when you confine yourself,
and look at the picture that retains something of his merit,
that retains something of that which you loved.

Do you remember, Marcus, that you brought
the famous Cyrenean painter from the proconsul's palace,
and he with an artist's guile
when he saw your friend, wished to persuade you
that he must represent him as Hyacinthus
(thus his picture would become more famous).

But Lanes would not lend his beauty thus;
and, firmly decided, he told the painter
to represent not Hyacinthus, nor anyone else,
but Lanes, son of Rametichus, of Alexandria.

(Unpublished draft from King's College, Cambridge)

The Tomb of Lanès [II]

The Lanès whom you loved is not here, Marcus,
in the tomb near which you come and weep, and remain
for hours and hours. You keep the Lanès whom you loved
nearer, when you confine yourself in your house
and look at the picture which somehow
has retained what was of value in him,
which somehow has retained what you loved.

Do you remember, Marcus, how you brought
the renowned Cyrenean painter from the proconsul's palace
and how cunningly he tried to persuade you both
when he saw your friend
that he should represent him as Hyacinthus
(so his picture would become more famous).

But Lanès would not lend his beauty thus;
and, firmly resisting, he told the painter
to represent not Hyacinthus, not anyone else,
but Lanès, son of Rametichus, Alexandrian.

(Unpublished draft from the Cavafy Archive)

The Tomb of Lysias the Grammarian

Close by, on the right, as you enter
the library of Berytus, we buried the learned Lysias,
the grammarian. The site is most fitting.
We laid him near the things that he remembers,
perhaps, even here—commentaries, texts, and technologies,
scripts, and many disquisitions on Greek idioms.
Here too his tomb will be seen and honoured
by us, when we pass on our way to the books.

(Unpublished draft from the Cavafy Archive)

Theodotus

You who are of the truly elect,
look narrowly how you acquire your predominance
whatever be your fame, however much
the cities of Italy and Thessaly
proclaim your achievements,
and your admirers at Rome
turn out in your favour honorary decrees:
neither your joy nor triumph will remain
nor will you regard yourself a superior person—superior indeed!—
when in Alexandria Theodotus brings you
upon a bloodstained charger
the wretched Pompey's head.

And do not flatter yourself that in your life,
circumscribed, well ordered, and prosaic,
there are no such dramatic and terrible things.
Perhaps at this very moment, into your neighbour's
well-ordered house, there enters—
unforeseen, impalpable—Theodotus
bearing just such another ghastly head.

(Published in *The Nation & The Athenaeum*, vol. 35, issue 6, 21 June 1924)

Those Who Fought for the Achaean League

Ye brave men who fought and died gloriously;
Ye who did not fear the ever victorious Romans.
Blameless ye, even if Diaeus and Critolaus erred.
When the Greeks shall wish to boast,
they shall say "Such men does our nation breed".
So wonderful will be the praise of you. —

These lines were written in Alexandria by an Achaean;
in the seventh year of Ptolemy Lathyrus.

(Unpublished draft from the Cavafy Archive)

To Antiochus Epiphanes[*]

The young Antiochian   said to the king
"In my heart there is   a cherished hope.
The Macedonians again,   Antiochus Epiphanes!
the Macedonians again,   are in the great struggle.
May they conquer!   and I shall give away willingly
the lion and the horses;   the coral statue of Pan;
the dainty palace;   and the gardens at Tyre;
and aught else you gave me,   oh, Antiochus Epiphanes".

Perhaps the King   was slightly moved.
But he suddenly remembered   a father and a brother
and he did not even reply.   An eavesdropper
could repeat some of his words.   Besides, as it was to be expected,
the disastrous end   soon came at Pydna.

(Published in *Échanges* 5 December 1931.)

---

[*]   According to the editors of *Échanges*, this poem was translated by C.P. Cavafy.

Voices

Voices ideal and beloved,
of those who are dead, or of those who,
for us, have disappeared like unto the dead.

Sometimes they speak in our dreams;
sometimes the mind hears them in our thoughts.

And they return for one moment with their sound
—the sound of poetry of our radiant years—
like distant music which fades away in the night.

(Unpublished draft from King's College, Cambridge)

When Julian Observed Much Lukewarmness

Considering then, that there is much lukewarmness
in respect of the Gods. — He says "lukewarmness"
in a grave manner. But after all, what can he expect?
Let him organise, as much as he pleases, a religious action,
let him write, as often as he likes, to the high-priest of Galadia,
or to the others such, exhorting them and guiding them.
We, his friends, are not Christians;
that much is clear. But in truth we cannot
play, like him— of the Nazarene brood—
at a new religious system,
ludicrous both in conception and in operation.
We are Greeks, after all — Nothing in excess, Oh Augustus!

(Published in *Échanges* 5 December 1931)

When They Wake Up

Try and keep them, poet,
however few are the visions
of your love-dream that you arrest.
Put them half veiled into your verses.
Try and keep them, poet,
when they wake up in your mind,
at night, or in the light of noon.

(Unpublished draft from King's College, Cambridge)

Young Men of Sidon (A.D. 400)

The actor whom they had brought to entertain them
recited, among other things, a few well chosen epigrams.

The room opened on to the garden,
and was pervaded with a faint scent of flowers,
which mingled with perfumes
of the five scented Sidonian young men.

He read verses of Meleager and Crinagoras and Rhianus.
But when he recited the lines:
"This monument covers Aeschylus, son of Euphorion, the Athenian . . ."
(emphasizing, perhaps a little too much
"stalwart valour" and "Marathonian grove")
an eager young man, who was a passionate lover of letters,
sprang up, and exclaimed:

"Oh! I do not care for these verses
such expressions savour somewhat of faintheartedness.
Let the great poet give — I say — to his art all his strength,
all his care, and again remember his art
in his adversity, or when his life is ebbing.
This I expect of him and demand;
and that he estrange not from his mind
the fine sense of Tragedy —
Agamemnon, admirable Prometheus,
the figures of Orestes and Cassandra,
the Seven against Thebes — and for the sake
of his memory he mentions only

that in the soldiers' ranks
he also fought against Datis and Artaphernes".

(Published in *Échanges* 5 December 1931)

Appendix

That the Mere Glimpse
by E.M. Forster [ca 1920]

I

That the mere glimpse of a plain cap
Could harry me with such longings,
Cause pain so dire!

That the mere glimpse of a plain coat
Could stab my heart with grief!
Enough! Take me with you to your home.

That a mere glimpse of plain leggings
Could tie my heart in tangles!
Enough! let us two be one.

2

In your lamb's wool and cuffs of leopard's fur
From people like me you hold aloof.
Of course I have other men:
But only you belong to old days.

In your lamb's wool and sleeves of leopard's fur
To people like me you are unfriendly.
Of course I have other men:
But it is only you I love.

(Unpublished draft from King's College, Cambridge)

To See a Sinadino Again[*]
by E.M. Forster, Weybridge, 29-1-24

To see a Sinadino again—
The thought fell into my heart like rain
And then began like a seed to sprout—
To see Alessandro coming out
Intent on lackadaisical sin—
Or Agostino going in
Sometimes flurried always worried
But never for one moment hurried—
Or Steffy the pride of all the three
—Too proud to feel safe when speaking to me—:—

Or even to know that—wherever I went—
A policeman's beat or a General's tent,
A brothel, a café, the Carvers' At Home,
Ramleh's remote and echoing dome,
The sea, when tepid, the streets, when cool,
The stairs, when dark, of a Greek girls' School
Always to know that wherever I go
I never know
When next I shall meet a Sinadino.

The thought has blossomed in exquisite flower,
And Alexandria returns for an hour.

(Unpublished draft from King's College, Cambridge)

---

[*]   The Sinadinos family was one of the preeminent mercantile families of the Alexandrian
      Greek community. Forster's poem features the sons of Michael Sinadinos, who served
      as president of the Greek Community during the war years.

To the Greek Poet C.P. Cavafy on his *Poiemata* (1908–1914)

By William Plomer

Your temple is built, without the least pretence,
On that antique foundation-stone, good sense,
A curious music fills its colonnades
And Attic sunbeams stripe the lofty shades,
Illumine quiet altars, and evoke
A warmth from marble and a form from smoke,
And show how the innermost recesses hold
Archaic trophies and Byzantine gold.

Voices of Asia and of Europe fuse
In the mad Russians and the vigorous Jews,
But you, Cavafy, more divinely speak
As your own blood spoke long ago, in Greek,
Wisdom and tears and tenderness and style
Blent in a subtle and nostalgic smile.

(Plomer's sonnet was published in his volume *The Fivefold Screen,* 1932)

Index